THE DAY AFTER

THE DAY AFTER

*A Retrospective on Religious Dissent
in the Presidential Crisis*

GABRIEL FACKRE

WILLIAM B. EERDMANS PUBLISHING COMPANY
GRAND RAPIDS, MICHIGAN / CAMBRIDGE, U.K.

© 2000 Wm. B. Eerdmans Publishing Co.
255 Jefferson Ave. S.E., Grand Rapids, Michigan 49503 /
P.O. Box 163, Cambridge CB3 9PU U.K.

Printed in the United States of America

05 04 03 02 01 00   7 6 5 4 3 2 1

Library of Congress Cataloging-in-Publication Data

Fackre, Gabriel J.
    The day after: a retrospective on religious dissent in the presidential crisis /
Gabriel Fackre.
        p.   cm.
    ISBN 0-8028-4713-7 (paper: alk. paper)
        1. Clinton, Bill, 1946 — Impeachment. 2. Clinton, Bill, 1946 — Religion.
    3. United States — Politics and government — 1993 — Moral and ethical
    aspects. 4. Christianity and politics — United States — History —
    20th century. 5. Religion and the press — United States — History —
    20th century. 6. Political corruption — United States — History —
    20th century. I. Title.

E886.2.F34   2000
973.929'092 — dc21
                                        99-057655

Contents

Introduction   1

1. A Small Saga   8

2. Clarifying the Conversations   17

3. Media Encounters   26

4. Ironies   43

5. Lessons   56

   Appendix: *"Declaration concerning Religion,
   Ethics, and the Crisis in the Clinton Presidency"*   75

Introduction

"The American people think . . ." and "the polls say . . ." have become mantras of end-century political commentary. Taking the temperature of the public and using it for policy decisions and talk show judgments are *de rigueur*. Yet such accommodation to the way things are does not pass without dissent. "No servility before the factual!" (Bonhoeffer) say some. And they draw on a long American tradition of countering cultural orthodoxies. *Religious* dissent has been a vital part of that Nay-saying heritage, from Pilgrim ancestors to a twentieth-century Martin King. Søren Kierkegaard gave forceful theological rationale for it in his attack on "the public," "the press," "the crowd," and "the Christian crowd" in nineteenth-century Denmark.[1] The argument of this book stands in this tradition.

The presidential impeachment proceedings were a showcase of the power of public opinion. "The polls," and "the American people" sent their message. The academy (as in the manifesto of

---

1. Søren Kierkegaard, *Attack on Christendom*, trans. Walter Lowrie (Boston: Beacon Press, 1956); Søren Kierkegaard, *The Present Age*, trans. Alexander Dru and Walter Lowrie (London: Oxford University Press, 1940).

900 historians) and my own Democratic party followed suit. "It's time to move on. . . . Forgive and forget. . . . Let's keep private and public separate. . . ." But dissent was also to be heard: "It's too soon to move on. . . . What about 'bearing fruit worthy of repentance?' . . . and the inseparability of the personal and the public?"

The impeachment controversies called forth an improbable company of religion teachers who set out a declaration, wrote a book, and promoted an electronic conversation at odds with public opinion and many of the opinion-makers. This is a case study of the whys and wherefores of that protest.

As editor of the book in question, *Judgment Day at the White House*,[2] I got an earful from old allies. "You used to *attack* the Religious Right[3] . . . were an avid *supporter* of Clinton.[4] Now you're a turncoat, part of a vast right-wing conspiracy!" Tough talk. Not to mention being accused in the press, along with the signers and authors, of being hard-edged "neo-Puritans," "sexual McCarthyites," "moralistic witch-hunters."

All this gives one pause. Many of us who are today's dissenters were also yesterday's protesters, marching in the civil rights struggles and peace movements of the 60s and 70s, and doing battle with an imperious "moral majority" and Religious Right in the 80s. Back then we scorned popular opinion and stood against "the establishment." But now not a few compatriots of that day are among our shrillest critics. Gone is their talk of hearkening "to the beat of a distant drummer." Instead, the end-

2. Gabriel Fackre, ed., *Judgment Day at the White House* (Grand Rapids: Eerdmans, 1999).

3. So Gabriel Fackre, *The Religious Right and Christian Faith* (Grand Rapids: Eerdmans, 1982).

4. As in the Associated Press story, February 7, 1993, in which I commend Clinton for his use of the book of Galatians in his first inaugural address and attempt to interpret his good theological intentions.

century saw old allies in lockstep with the polls and the Powers That Be.

Of course, "new occasions teach new duties." Different contexts may call for varying political postures. More about that down the page. But the fundamental moral norms of truth and justice remain the same. So does the call to listen to the one Word and to protest the manipulation of faith. When occasions of moral and religious outrage recur, old duties continue as new ones.

In that same pause one remembers the accusations hurled at the dissenters of another day: "You are part of the left-wing conspiracy . . . a front for the communists!" The demagogue tarred the opposition with that brush, associating it with a public enemy, deflecting attention from the merits of the case. It worked well for a while. But then came the rejoinder: "Guilt by association!" And finally that countercharge sank in. "McCarthyism" became its despised synonym.

But now the old rhetoric resurfaces. Here comes "conspiracy" again, but this time it's "the vast right-wing conspiracy." And the role reversal brings with it a natural companion, in Alan Dershowitz's phrase, "sexual McCarthyism." But how is this not "guilt by association"? How not the same kind of demagoguery? One, ironically, deployed by a Left that suffered its cruelties in a time too quickly forgotten.

"Right" and "Left." . . . The country's underlying crisis has been diagnosed as a battle between a *cultural* Right and Left.[5] And somewhere in the ranks of each army are to be found (front-and-center or in the rear echelons, depending on the ob-

5. As in Robert Wuthnow, *Restructuring of American Religion* (Princeton: Princeton University Press, 1990) and *The Struggle for the American Soul* (Grand Rapids: Eerdmans, 1989), and James Davison Hunter, *Culture Wars* (New York: Basic Books, 1992) and *Before the Shooting Begins* (New York: The Free Press, 1994).

server) the Religious Right and Religious Left. The hot-button issues of abortion and homosexuality are often the triggering mechanisms of mutual bombardment. But a range of controversies is included: the role of government, the ownership of guns, the conflict between tree-huggers and tree-cutters, the choice between protection of environment or jobs, the build-up or close-down of the military, prayer in or out the public schools, a downtown crèche or a naked public square. In sum, James Carville vs. James Dobson. Or as some would have it, the dividing line between modernism and anti-modernism, presaged by the first monkey trial and now apparent in the warfare between the agile relativist Bill Clinton and the doddering absolutist Henry Hyde.[6] The future of the country, we are told, will be decided by this contest. The question is that of the old union song: "Which side are you on . . . which side are you on?" This culture-war theory, indeed, became the presidential explanation for the impeachment proceedings: rabid Republicans using Congress to defeat the Constitution and its defenders.[7]

Is this Manichaean reading of the present crisis right? Either in the surface debates about impeachment or the deeper questions of cultural division? The give-and-take described in this book tells another story. A simplistic culture-war theory does not fit the picture. The tale is about an elusive "center" not easily identified with either camp.[8] Given its sharp critiques, it is hardly a "mushy middle" unable to make up its mind, or a "mid-

6. As in Frank Rich, *Op-Ed*, "Inherit the Wind," *New York Times*, January 20, 1999, A31.

7. President Clinton on the "lessons" of the impeachment in his interview with Dan Rather on *Sixty Minutes* 2, March 31, 1999.

8. On such a center, see Kyle A. Pasewark and Garrett E. Paul, "Forming an Emphatic Christian Center: A Call to Political Responsibility," *The Christian Century* 111 (August 24-31, 1994): 780-83. See also Douglas Jacobsen and William Vance Trollinger, Jr., "Evangelical and Ecumenical: Re-forming the Center," *The Christian Century* 111 (July 13-20, 1994): 682-84.

dle way" always predictably steering a safe mediating course. And this center is defined by religious commitments, not political alliances.

For Christians the orientation point is, with Dietrich Bonhoeffer, "Christ the Center."[9] That polestar enables a "church of the Center"[10] to move in freedom across the spectrum of current allegiances, deriving its judgments from its own norms and not from political partisanships. Freedom from ideology may move one to the left or to the right on a given issue, prompting marches for social justice in one context and a stand for personal virtue in another. Because of a "seamless" personal/public ethics, it may cause a company of Clinton supporters to call for the president's resignation, refuting the claim of fellow-Democrats that the whole thing is simply a Republican vendetta.

The freedom of Declaration signers to deviate from political expectations, and the rejection of a modulated both/and centrism, prompted sharp criticism of another sort. We were faulted for not calling Starr and his investigation to account. Of course, *Judgment Day at the White House* includes six chapters that do just that in one way or another, with a number of essayists providing a counterpoint to the Declaration. However, the Declaration and its interpreters chose to focus on the religio-moral questions explicitly posed by the president's words and actions because it was precisely these matters that "the American people," the polls, political partisans, and too much of the religious community appeared to dismiss with their calls to "move on." We do speak of "The Starr pruriencies,"[11] but rather than echo

9. Dietrich Bonhoeffer, *Christ the Center* (New York: Harper & Row, 1966).

10. On this phenomenon see the writer's *Restoring the Center: Essays Evangelical and Ecumenical* (Downers Grove, Ill.: InterVarsity Press, 1998), pp. 27-45.

11. *Judgment Day at the White House*, p. 102.

the conventional wisdom, we sought to speak a word unspoken in our own ranks; we especially wanted to distinguish ourselves on matters of personal morality from "the war cries of the Religious Right."[12]

In what follows, the role of the media and the polls is taken up. Can we learn something about religious dissent from this encounter with Kierkegaard's "public," "press," "crowd," and "Christian crowd"? For those who attempt to *influence* all of the above by posting a Declaration on the Internet and writing a volume for a hoped-for wider *public,* and who want fair treatment from the *press,* Kierkegaard's simple scorn for "the masses" is unacceptable. His indictment was also the disdain of an aristocrat for a society that dissolved "the individual." Dissent that honors democracy is selective in its disavowals, speaking its "No" to a partisan press, an apathetic public, and a theologically confused and morally silent church. Its focus is on reminding itself and its co-believers of common commitments. In the public square its declarations and doings are attempts to awaken sleeping giants to their own professed loyalties. It will stand against the press, the government, the crowd, and the Christian crowd when the one Word, Jesus Christ, tells dissenters that they cannot do otherwise.

While "religious dissent" is our refrain, the dissenters in question are almost all confessing Christians. When the Declaration was originally conceived, the phrase "religious scholars" was used intentionally, and the content of the Declaration formulated in broadly religious rather than Christian-specific terms. The hope was that its signers might include non-Christians. The latter did not materialize, except for a few supporters late in the struggle.[13] All the authors in *Judgment Day at the*

12. *Judgment Day at the White House,* p. ix.
13. One of them was Jacob Neusner.

White House are Christian, and many of the interpretations of the role of religion and morality discussed in that volume are based on Christian premises, as are those of its critics. So too is the theology in this work. It is the kind of theology that affirms points of convergence between Christian faith and other religions in matters moral and political, based on an understanding of "common grace" that enables conversation and collegiality across worldview lines.[14] But these shared warrants are deeply embedded in the particulars of Christian teaching, within the framework of which "religious dissent" is here interpreted.

The investigation opens with a chapter that positions the reader on the underside of the episode, viewing it from the vantage point of developing dissent. Chapter 2 makes a distinction between two conversations, a distinction that has not been sufficiently recognized in popular commentary, political or religious. Chapter 3 looks at the twentieth-century version of Kierkegaard's press, but with a discriminating lens. Chapter 4 takes up 1998-1999 illustrations of "the irony of American history."[15] Chapter 5 examines some lessons that can be drawn from end-century events, with the accent on theological learnings.

---

14. On "common grace," see the writer's *The Doctrine of Revelation: A Narrative Interpretation* (Grand Rapids: Eerdmans, 1997), pp. 61-67.

15. So Reinhold Niebuhr, *The Irony of American History* (New York: Macmillan, 1982).

Chapter 1

A Small Saga

We begin with a flashback. In May of 1973, the press began to take notice of increasingly vocal criticism of "White House religion." President Nixon had long courted religious figures, using them to conduct services in the White House, prompting subsequent glowing testimonies to the president's piety. Billy Graham, America's then best-known religious name, was a frequent visitor to, and spiritual adviser of, the president. But Watergate was now upon us. *Other* religious voices were being heard. An Associated Press story reported that

> As Watergate unfolds, moral theologians cite a kind of "White House religion" — a personalized piety detached from its social demands — as a factor in the affair."[1]

Episcopal leader John Coburn declared, "Watergate implies not so much a 'constitutional crisis' as a 'moral crisis' in the country."[2] William Sloan Coffin objected to Nixon minions using religion "to cover up wrongdoing."[3] A Gannett religion writer

1. Associated Press, July 14, 1973.
2. Associated Press, July 14, 1973.
3. Associated Press, July 14, 1973.

urged that "Nixon Needs New Religious Advisers," suggesting the friends of Reinhold Niebuhr rather than the consorts of Graham and Norman Vincent Peale.[4] In the midst of presidential scandal and the threat of impeachment, church leaders announced a "moral crisis" and protested "the use and abuse of religion." The Gannett writer was the drafter of the declaration on "White House religion" to which the AP story referred.[5]

Now twenty-six years later came the same concerns about "White House religion." Once again they appeared amidst the sound and fury of yet another impeachment crisis. Indeed the same language of "moral crisis" was heard.[6] And the same charges about religion used to "cover up wrongdoing" were hurled. But today we have a different cast of characters.

While the end-century presidential crisis had been developing since January 1998 accusations of acts of sexual misconduct in the White House, it was not until the "prayer breakfast" of September 11, 1998, that the religious aspect became high profile. On that occasion, several hundred clergy and other religious leaders were invited to a White House morning meal. The president's remarks included an acknowledgment of wrongdoing and a plea for forgiveness. They were greeted with resounding applause, with many testimonies after the event to the sincerity of his declarations.

About the same time, President Clinton also appeared before an African-American congregation to speak about repen-

---

4. Ross Blake, "Ponderings," Gannett News Service, May 12, 1973.

5. "We view the Watergate scandal as a call to national repentance for the arrogance of power and the apathy of the citzenry. . . . A White House religion that insulates the leaders of government from the prophetic Word cohabits with a White House ethics of deceit and dishonesty." *Watergate and Evangelism*, UCC clergy and laity.

6. The name of the web site of the Declaration signatories, "Religion, Ethics and the Crisis in the Clinton Presidency," http://www.moral-crisis.org.

tance and forgiveness. He also met with Jesse Jackson on the matter, enlisted Tony Campolo, Gordon MacDonald, and Philip Wogaman to be his "spiritual advisers," and sent a letter to his Southern Baptist congregation in Arkansas. The religious endorsements of presidential contrition were concomitant with a growing national mood: "It's time to move on . . . to forgive and forget."

Taking all of this in were two biblical scholars, Robert Jewett of Garrett-Evangelical Theological Seminary and Klyne Snodgrass of North Park Seminary, later joined by another guild member, David Scholer of Fuller Theological Seminary. Several days after the president's prayer breakfast, Jewett sent a manuscript to Snodgrass in which he compared the co-opting of a religious leader for political purposes in biblical history (Jehonadab by Jehu) to circumstances in the White House.[7] He posed the question: How do the various biblical texts and teachings on repentance and forgiveness relate to the president's take on these subjects . . . and the clergy endorsements of the same? There was a serious clash here of understandings of repentance. Snodgrass responded enthusiastically and suggested that the contents might be the germ of a "manifesto" from religious scholars who shared these concerns. The Jewett paper was further circulated, with Scholer giving active encouragement. Meanwhile Snodgrass drafted an initial version of a developing "declaration" that was e-mailed to a widening circle of colleagues. University of Chicago professor Don Browning, who had just expressed his views in a letter to *The Christian Century*, provided important feedback. Jewett did a second draft in the light of responses, with revisions done in consultation with Snodgrass and Professor Jean Bethke Elshtain, political philoso-

7. Later published as "The Prayer Breakfast Confession," *Pro Ecclesia* 7, no. 4 (Fall 1998): 395-97.

pher at the University of Chicago and writer for the *New Republic*. Jewett, together with colleagues Snodgrass and Scholer, made plans for an Internet web site designed to explore the issues raised by the Declaration. Further, they contacted publisher William B. Eerdmans, Jr., with the hope that a book of essays on the Declaration might be put together. Eerdmans endorsed the project, and staff member Reinder van Til became a key intermediary, house editor, and supporter of the developing project.

The Declaration reached its final form in late October and by November 13 had accumulated 87 signers. (The number reached 192 in the Spring of 1999.) A search was mounted for a technically adept person to set up a web site that would aid discussion of the Declaration, list its signatories, provide information about the developing book, and appeal for financial support to get the Declaration publicized. The webmaster position was filled by Douglas Harrison, a student at the University of Southern California, and committees were appointed to oversee the content; a volunteer steering group was organized to make general policy decisions.

The word began to get out. Jewett was interviewed in a PBS *Religion & Ethics NewsWeekly* series and Elshtain appeared on a CNN call-in program. Religion writer Kenneth Woodward found the developments newsworthy and did a short piece in the November 23, 1998, *Newsweek*, "Should the President Be Forgiven?" quoting from the Declaration and citing some of its signers. The following week, "Bill Clinton's Ethics and Ours" appeared on the *Wall Street Journal* op-ed page with the full text of the Declaration and some of its signatories. The Religious News Service did a November story, subsequently cited by both *The Christian Century* and *Christianity Today*. Interestingly, the Declaration was linked in the story to a statement issued "under the aegis of the Institute on Religion and Democracy," with signers "a group of clerics and religious leaders, most of them related to conservative causes,"[8] a connection that the *Century*, editorially critical of the Declaration, was pleased to note. *Christianity Today*, editorially critical of Clinton for the opposite reason, also took pains to record this fact.

The result of this early exposure was an inquiry from some of Jewett's local friends as to whether funds might be raised for an advertisement that would give the Declaration further visibility in the mainstream press. Money was given by these volunteers and from others, including Declaration signers; ads appeared subsequently in the January 9, 1999, *Washington Post* and in the January 12 *New York Times*.

The book, now with a name, *Judgment Day at the White House*, and the Declaration, began a new phase of joint public exposure, a "coming out party" at the annual meetings of the largest assembly of religious scholars in the nation — the American Academy of Religion and the Society for Biblical Literature — the November 1998 gathering in Orlando, Florida. Jewett proposed that a forum be held at Orlando on the volume and the Declaration. As Philip Wogaman, pastor of the church in Washington attended by the Clintons, was known to have a book forthcoming on the same issues *(From the Eye of the Storm)*,[9] why not have a debate between a *Judgment Day* contributor and Wogaman? Efforts were begun to find a voice for our views, going through a list of Elshtain, Fackre, Stackhouse, and Hauerwas, none of whom were available. Jewett stepped in at the last minute to represent the Declaration and our collection. Meanwhile, Wogaman agreed to participate, and was flown in by the cooperative efforts of Eerdmans and Westminster/John Knox, Wogaman's publisher. In spite of many competing meetings on

8. "Scholars Criticize Calls to Forgive Clinton," *The Christian Century* 115, no. 33 (December 2, 1998): 1138.

9. J. Philip Wogaman, *From the Eye of the Storm: A Pastor to the President Speaks Out* (Philadelphia: Westminster/John Knox Press, 1999).

the same night, an overflow crowd of 300 was on hand for the lively exchange.

The Book

The coming to be of *Judgment Day at the White House* is a story in itself. The idea for a collection of essays on the presidential crisis took shape at a meal following a late-September lecture at Fourth Presbyterian Church in Chicago, a meal that included lecturer Elshtain, Reinder van Til, Jewett, and Snodgrass. Recruited as editor shortly after, and with suggestions for contributors from publisher Eerdmans, I consulted with Jewett and Snodgrass about writers, pro and con. We came up with some names from the list of signers for the former and from e-mail declensions for the latter. I contacted prospects in early October by e-mail and phone. We received predictable turn-downs because of the demanding deadline ("send by November 15!"), and in some cases institutional considerations (possible offense given to constituencies). A rejection slip had to go from the editor to one contributor: "No, an old sermon on the subject will not do." But then a remarkable flow of essays began to materialize, all but one on schedule. In fact, we had an abundance of riches that kept extending the length of the book well beyond its original 100+ pages to its final length of 200, with Mr. Eerdmans agreeing to retain the original 100-page price of twelve dollars. We placed the Elshtain essay as lead-off, for it captured the Declaration spirit so well and was crafted with the skill of a *New Republic* writer. A natural sequel were chapters by two of the country's best-known ethicists, Max Stackhouse of Princeton and Stanley Hauerwas of Duke (frequently at odds with one another elsewhere but both signatories of the Declaration). Boston College's Matthew Lamb's articulate Roman Catholic perspective followed, with the "Letter to the Editor" of the *Christian Century* by Don Browning and an essay by Morningside College philosopher John Lawrence rounding out the section on "the Ethics and Politics of Repentance and Forgiveness." A set of essays organized themselves naturally into the next section, for they drew on disciplines partner to ethics and politics and did it with detailed documentation. I clustered the three biblical essays, with Jewett's research (with 72 endnotes) as lead-off, followed by the careful exegetical chapters of co-organizer Snodgrass and St. Xavier University professor Troy Martin. Next came an essay by Edward Wimberly of the Interdenominational Center in Atlanta, drawing on his tradition of black theology and counseling expertise to argue for the integrity of personal and public morality. My own piece concluded the section with an attempt to make the case for personal/public interrelationships from classical Christian doctrine.

Six hefty essays stated the counter-position. House editor van Til wisely moved Yale professor Nicholas Wolterstorff's piece to the lead position, for it challenged, in turn, each of the six Declaration points. Pittsburgh Seminary's John Burgess followed, arguing that in the Clinton case "truth matters more than justice." Retired Fuller professor Lewis Smedes faulted the Declaration for not taking into account the more important issue of social justice. Georgetown's William Buckley (not to be confused with the notable William F.), while sympathetic with many of the Declaration's concerns, used the Roman Catholic catechetical tradition to argue otherwise. Fuller ethicist Glenn Stassen, as did Smedes, questioned the Declaration's exclusive concern with private matters. Donald Shriver, former president of Union Seminary, and his spouse Peggy, leader in the National Council of Churches, struck similar notes.

The remaining sections of the book included republished essays by well-known thinkers and commentators: Stephen Carter and Shelby Steele (taking positions at odds with many other African-American leaders) and Andrew Sullivan, expressing views similar to those of the Declaration. The last section included the speeches of President Clinton in August and September, to which the Declaration alluded.

Judgment Day at the White House appeared in mid-December 1998 and began to make its way to manifold outlets through the labors of the Eerdmans publicity department. Among them were all the members of the House Judiciary Committee, then later the full House, and even later the full Senate. Ads appeared in the *New Republic, The Weekly Standard,* and in religious publications such as *The Christian Century.*

The results? The media response is discussed and evaluated below. Suffice to say here that the reception for a religious book was unusual, including Senate phone calls and citations in Congress, interviews and reviews by newspaper chains and radio and television network programs, all in the space of a few weeks after publication. And the anger generated by it was notable, including a string of anonymous hate calls to the editor and publisher.

During and after the congressional proceedings, the Declaration and *Judgment Day at the White House* were discussed in public assemblies around the country, in churches, and in political fora. High profile was a Chicago debate between Philip Wogaman and Jean Bethke Elshtain at Fourth Presbyterian Church attended by 900 people, a give-and-take repeated on Ted Koppel's *Nightline* program a few days later. Snodgrass and Martin defended the Declaration in an exchange with three critics at Wheaton College that same evening. Jewett also debated Wogaman in a forum at Washington's Wesley Seminary where the latter teaches. The web site continued to be visited by thousands each month and articles posted on the issues, pro and con. The first wave of reviews and stories that appeared in the

popular media tapered off, but a second wave began and continues in religious journals, together totaling over fifty in the first
six months. The return by the public ever and again to "presidential affairs" prompted by Monica Lewinsky's reappearance in
book and television interviews, and by George Stephanopolis's
in-house critique of his former boss, *All Too Human*, kept alive
the concerns of the Declaration and tended to confirm its judgments, as did the report on White House damage-control tech-
niques by former White House lawyer Lanny Davis in *Truth to
Tell*. But the "let's move on" of earlier days finally took hold, and
the pundits who reveled in daily commentary had to find other
subject matter. However, the religious issues in the presidential
crisis will not go away. As we shall argue in the chapters that follow, they are perennial, and the small saga through which we
lived is a laboratory of learning about moral and theological ba-
sics.

Chapter 2

Clarifying the Conversations

C ontributing to the cacophony surrounding the presidential crisis was the confusion of two different conversations. There were points of convergence, but the divergences were consequential. Failure to recognize the latter obscured vital matters whatever the forum — congressional inquiry, pundit commentary, or pulpit declamation. What suffered particularly from the fusion of the two was attention to the "religious" distinctives of *Conversation 1*.

Conversation 1

Critical to Conversation 1 was the dialogue between those who shared President Clinton's religious language and concerns. It was triggered by the president's public acts of penitence — the 1998 prayer breakfast of clergy and religious leaders, his letter to his Southern Baptist congregation in Little Rock, Arkansas, and professions before an African-American congregation, the defense of the president by his Washington pastor, Philip Wogaman, his soliciting of spiritual counsel from the Reverends Jesse

Jackson, Tony Campolo, and Gordon MacDonald (who, inciden-
tally, had resigned from his congregation because of an affair, but
had been reinstated).[1]

In Conversation 1, most of the president's interlocutors
were fellow-Christians. Hearing professions of penitence, seeing
the settings in which he made them and the clergy who sanc-
tioned them, they asked: What is the meaning of repentance?
Where and when is it fitting? How is repentance related to forgiveness? What is the relation of personal to public morality?
Do the ten commandments — in this case the seventh and
ninth, about adultery and false witness — have a bearing on
public office? How can we hold together the importance of both
social justice and personal virtue? Must we sacrifice one to the
other? What are the moral responsibilities of a Christian in public office? What is the relation of religion, the Christian faith in
particular, to a specific political agenda? Profound issues long reflected upon in the Christian tradition were set squarely in the
public forum by this crisis. Here was an invitation to dialogue.

The signers of the Declaration and authors of *Judgment Day
at the White House* responded. The manifesto and the book are,
first and foremost, a voice in Conversation 1, part of a distinctly
religious exchange. The categories are repentance and forgiveness, how faith functions in the public square, what the moral
norms are for a person of faith in public office. While this conversation does have political implications (what the president
and his coreligionists might or might not do if persuaded by critical commentary), the president's interlocutors are *not* in this

---

1. Gordon MacDonald writes about ministering to the strayed in *Re-
building Your Broken World* (New York: Thomas Nelson, 1998). For a review
that criticizes this book and Wogaman's *From the Eye of the Storm* for their
"liberal Protestant" illusions (although MacDonald is a professed evangelical),
see Jean Bethke Elshtain, "God and Man in the Oval Office," *The New Republic*
no. 4392 (March 22, 1999): 37-40.

mode addressing political organs or constitutional tribunals. This conversation is *not* about impeachment or removal from office by the investigatory procedures of an independent counsel, the House of Representatives, or the Senate. While these procedures, in fact, are the context of Conversation 1 and lend it an urgency, the same dialogue would be entirely appropriate without the dealings of Kenneth Starr, Barney Frank, and Henry Hyde. "Believers" who heard and saw kindred professions want a word with a president and his supporters who share with them the language and commitments of faith. The government is not invited into this exchange. It has to do with the state of the heart, the mouth and the hands and feet *coram Deo* — "before God" — not in front of an earthly tribunal. The *theological* and the *legal*, therefore, are distinguishable concerns.

When heavenly and earthly tribunals are mistakenly fused, two conversations are confused. Conversation 1 is merged into a second yet to be considered: "Conversation 2" — a dialogue with a much wider constituency, different venues, and distinct standards appropriate to earthly tribunals ("treason, high crimes and misdemeanors," etc.). In the culture war that accompanied the crisis, the partisans on both sides made this mistake. The "Right," especially the "Religious Right," too often introduced, sub rosa, the criteria of the first conversation into the second. Thus rigorous religious-specific and Christian-specific norms of personal morality and repentance were tacitly at work as criteria for deciding matters of impeachment and removal from office. The "Left," especially the "Religious Left," rejected this identification, but then sharply separated *any* consideration of more generalized standards of personal morality from Conversation 2 and matters appropriate to the earthly tribunal. (At least in theory, for one of the ironies to be later discussed was the campaign for a vote of congressional censure on precisely these grounds by many who declared personal behavior off limits to government scrutiny.) The Right could turn Conversation 2 into Conversation 1 and its criteria. The Left could turn Conversation 1 into Conversation 2 and its criteria.[2] We need here a "center" that can make *distinctions* but avoid *separations*.

An obvious subject of Conversation 1 is, "What is repentance?" And fast on its heels, "What is forgiveness?" Entailed in both: "How are they understood in the Bible so prominently displayed in the president's hand on exiting from Sunday services?" "How illumined are they by the Christian tradition in which he stands?" In the exchange about these matters, it is appropriate for the president to say to his critics, "I'm doing everything I'm supposed to do . . . before God. I've said I'm sorry. I have repented. I've got my spiritual counselors. I'm trying to get back to doing the nation's business. What more do you want?" *Christian Century* editor James Wall made the same kind of case in his editorial "Come on Down!" With altar call background, he finds the penitent president "down front" making his confession. But he's waiting there for the rest of us: What about all you self-righteous critics with your own sins? Come on down!

In that give-and-take, there will be a response. To Clinton: "Grace is *free*, but it is not *cheap*. Repentance that receives the divine mercy is a turn-around, deeds done as well as words spoken. Let's 'walk the walk' as well as 'talk the talk.' For a Christian who is the most powerful person in the country (world?), making amends for things done is big time. To whom much is given much is required." To Wall: "Here we are down front . . . with editor and president. Let's each do something as well as say something that relates to why we're here. Let the self-imposed penance be commensurate with who we are and what we've

2. The moves of both parties on personal morality looked strikingly similar to those rejected by the Council of Chalcedon on the issue of the Person of Christ. The Monophysites fused the natures and the Nestorians separated them.

done; let the 'punishment fit the crime.' " More about the exchange with *The Christian Century* later.

What are the premises of Clinton's religious critics? At work in the above comments is a Christian tradition on the meaning of repentance to be discussed in Chapter 5. Here we anticipate. Repentance, *metanoia*, is a threefold movement: contrition of the heart, confession of the mouth, satisfaction by the hands and feet. True contrition of the heart is known only to God. Confession of the mouth is a public act. Whether it's made or not is empirically discernible. The Declaration's references to "incomplete repentance" presuppose the importance of the third movement, actions that show the seriousness of what the lips say and the heart feels.

And forgiveness? "Grace is free," a fundamental teaching. We are not saved by our works, since "no one . . . is righteous, not even one" (Romans 3:10). We count on the mercy of God, enacted in the life, death, and resurrection of Christ. We are saved by grace . . . received in faith. Grace is free but it is *not* cheap, as Dietrich Bonhoeffer rightly argued.[3] The act of a receiving faith entails a turn-around repentance and new obedience. Reception of free grace requires more than "confession of the mouth." We are back to the meaning of repentance and will return to the subject in more detail in the chapter on lessons learned.

Another piece of the religious conversation is the question, "What is the proper relation of faith to the stewardship by Christians of political power? What of the charge that religion is ideology, a smokescreen for our interests? Does not the gathering of clergy in a White House venue in order to hear and approve a confession of wrongdoing that puts one in political jeop-

---

3. Dietrich Bonhoeffer, *The Cost of Discipleship*, trans. R. H. Fuller and Irmgard Booth (New York: Macmillan, 1960), pp. 35-47.

ardy raise questions about the use of faith? And the relation of faith not only to the powers that be, but also to the people? Is public opinion, the *vox populi,* one and the same as *vox Dei?"* And then the questions long-discussed in Christian theology and ethics: "What is the place of morality — personal or public — in the realm of the state and the custodians of its power?" And the final question of consequences: "What does repentance that issues in making amends for wrongdoing involve vis-à-vis those that have been wronged, especially so in the public sector?"

The questions posed in Conversation 1 are addressed to the president and his supporters and have to do with decisions he makes, or they make. They are a fundamental part of the Declaration and *Judgment Day at the White House.*

Conversation 2

Conversation 2 is about constitutional, legal, and political matters. The decision-makers here are members of Congress weighing the impeachment and removal of the president from office. The criteria for decision-making are the officially stipulated ones: "treason, . . . high crimes and misdemeanors." The evidence put forward for the latter is not breach of religious faith or violation of its rigorous moral norms, but rather material germane to the stipulations. Hence, public data relative to perjury, abuse of power, and obstruction of justice as arguable evidence for constitutional breaches become focal in this forum. Here we have to do with standards of judgment that are in important ways different from those in Conversation 1. Here also is a different venue for adjudicating the issues, and a different circle of discussants.

The decisions that are made as *outcome* of this conversation are, finally, by *others*, not by the president. The action taken is, finally, by the state and its duly constituted organs. The judgment bar is made of human materials. The "day of judgment" is on our calendars — a penultimate reckoning. Judgment Day is divine chronology — an ultimate assize.

For all that, moral matters taken up in Conversation 1 are not *excluded* from Conversation 2. While not Christian-specific, or norms of any other identifiable religious tradition, the charges of lying, abuse of power, and obstruction of justice are *moral* issues. So too the "high crimes and misdemeanors" to which they must conform to be impeachable offenses. From its inception, the United States has written moral universals into its charters and codes. Whatever their historical sources (eighteenth-century Enlightenment premises? Judeo-Christian principles? the "free church" protest against the agglomeration of power, religious and secular?), they are general guidelines for behavior in public office. In Christian theological terms, the awareness of the unacceptability of stealing, murder, lying, coveting, etc. is variously characterized as the gift of "natural law," "universal moral law," "common grace," "general revelation." God gives the world enough universal light in conscience and corporate sensibilities to restrain the chaos that comes from the Fall, enough to make human life together livable. Of course, the foregoing "thou shalt nots" are found also in Scripture as part of the second table of the Ten Commandments. Theologically, "general revelation" and "special revelation" overlap at the point of rudimentary moral behavior.

Because of the overlap, Conversation 1 and Conversation 2 also converge at the point of moral accountability. Hence, the Declaration and *Judgment Day at the White House* are also addressed to the general public. They have to do with conduct arguably appropriate in a public office accountable to national charters and codes. As the Declaration puts it, there is a moral "threshold" below which occupants of public office should not fall, especially so the resident of the House of the people. Thus a pattern of lying in a public office responsible for the welfare of a people and affecting the fate of nations is a breach of rudimentary moral law and invites the chaos it is designed to restrain. Both the specifics of Christian teaching and the fundaments of public weal require elemental personal moral qualities.

Because the Declaration and *Judgment Day at the White House* were addressed to the general public engaged in Conversation 2 as well as the religious public involved in Conversation 1, the widest possible fora were sought. Hence the ads in secular media, the welcome of public discussion, and the distribution of the book to the members of Congress during the hearings. The caption of the ads in *The New York Times* and *The Washington Post* read: "The personal and the political are inseparable." Of course, the "religious public" is also part of the general public, and, therefore, the general media are vehicles for communicating the issues of Conversation 1 as well.

To sharpen the distinction of conversations, while recognizing at the same time their overlap in political consequences, the clarification may be made this way: Conversation 1 is theological. Those launching it strive to make their case with others who share their fundamental religious premises. The intended outcome could be the resignation of the president. Such might come about because of Clinton's own religious convictions (as an act of making amends). Or it could be precipitated by the influence of coreligionists convinced by the critique.

Conversation 2 is legal. It was launched by the Starr investigation and is carried out in constitutional venues and in the general public, based on constitutional criteria. Its consequences are constitutionally stipulated: impeachment or removal from office, or nonimpeachment and nonremoval from office.

When these distinctions are recognized, it is clear that one could argue *for* resignation as the outcome of Conversation 1 and argue *against* impeachment and removal from office as the outcome of Conversation 2. And that was the view of one group of those who signed the Declaration and contributed essays defending it in *Judgment Day at the White House.* One also might argue for *both* or *neither,* and each had their constituencies in both documents.

The inclusion of a number of critics of the Declaration in the book published to advocate it, and the invitation to dialogue in the Declaration and on the web site, represented attempts to show that religious dissent of this sort in this crisis was not an ideological crusade that had no time for other points of view. They were instead serious attempts at "conversation." Indeed, the need for *two* of them.

Chapter 3

Media Encounters

In a secular society, "religion" struggles to get the public's attention. Mainline religion, declared now to be "sideline," craves it more than most, especially so in its desire to affect social change. Suddenly, however, in the presidential crisis, the mainline found itself in "the eye of the storm." Ironically, it was the religious take on matters of *personal* morality, so little stressed publically by the mainline, that gained a hearing for the church and other religious voices. (The saga is full of ironies, others to be subsequently explored.) How did this interest in religious opinion play out in the newly attentive media? We examine three expressions of the same vis-à-vis the Declaration and its supporting efforts: "friendly," "fair," and "foul." And then take a look at an in-house give-and-take among mainliners.

"Friendly"

Earliest media attention came from *Newsweek*, *The Wall Street Journal*, and *The Washington Times*, duly noted on the Rush Limbaugh radio program. It's not hard to figure out why. Each had an ax to grind. Hence "friendly" is in quotes, as in other circumstances and on other issues, many of the dissenters would be on an "enemy" list. Kenneth Woodward, religion editor of *Newsweek*, had written articles critical of Clinton. *The Wall Street Journal* was glad to have support for its views on Clinton from "religious scholars." And *The Washington Times*, with pronounced conservative sympathies, took delight in the number of Democrats disillusioned with Clinton. Limbaugh's views were predictable.

Woodward's "Should the President Be Forgiven?" (November 23, 1998) cited the "strongly worded" Declaration that criticized the prayer breakfast as a "transparent effort to elicit religious 'authentication of a politically motivated and incomplete repentance.'" Woodward saw it as a "voice of religious dissent to the presidential hymn of forgiveness." *The Wall Street Journal* printed the Declaration in its entirety (November 30, 1998), listing six of its well-known signatories (P. Achtemeier, Donfried, Elshtain, Hauerwas, Stackhouse, and Yeide). *The Washington Times* (December 26, 1998) captioned its piece "Ethicists who supported Clinton fault his moral posture," quoting the writer and Robert Jewett as disappointed by the lockstep support of Clinton by fellow-Democrats and criticizing the "cheap forgiveness" and "polls morality" at work. *The Times* also cited *Judgment Day at the White House*, mentioning the inclusion of opponents of the Declaration and citing the views of one of them, Lewis Smedes.

In the category of "friendly," but now of religious not secular stripe, were invitations to appear on "Christian radio" talk programs. On two occasions the writer fielded thirty minutes of questions from Michigan and Ohio stations with sympathetic hosts, but callers not always so inclined.

It was not lost upon the early Declaration signers and those writing supportive essays in the book that both secular and religious media visibility was sometimes itself subject to manipulation by Clinton critics and from political and religious persuasions unlike many of their own. Prompting even more unease was air time given by what we found to be chronic "Clinton haters." Several Internet meetings featuring Clinton scandal added the book to its reading lists. And the writer, agreeing with some ambivalence to be a guest on a talk show of the "American Freedom Network," found himself between commercials for survivalist kits and right-wing books stressing his Democratic party affiliation and mainline church identity. Here were lessons in how the critics of manipulation must themselves guard against the same.

Fair

Is it possible for the media presentation of the issues at hand to treat this controversial subject with "objectivity"? Objectivity is *out* in many places in our postmodern times when reporting and historiography are seen to be only socially located power-driven partisanship. While recognizing that finitude and sin do work their ways on all reportage without acceding to today's pop relativism, one can hope for an approximation of "fair play." Better this than even professedly "friendly" outlets, given the latter's obvious agendas. We found a measure of it with some journalists and some radio and TV interviewers.

Sandi Dolbee is an officer of the Religion Writers Association. The trust of her colleagues is warranted. Her independent report on the Declaration and *Judgment Day at the White House* for the San Diego *Union Tribune* was a model of fair play. Captioned "A Judgment Call: A new book examines both sides of Clinton's redemptive journey," the article understood our attempt to create a forum of differing opinion in the midst of culture-war polarizations. At the same time, Dolbee reported the main thrust of the volume to be a critique of "moral confusion and religious manipulation" based on the earlier Declaration.

She quoted representative paragraphs from the book, citing in proportion from the pro and con sections, and she was meticulous in honoring the specifics of the interview with the writer. The article was the first-page feature of the "People" section on Saturday, January 2, 1999, with an accompanying picture of Clinton leaving church with the ever-present Bible. It is hard to tell from the story where Dolbee's own sympathies lay.

More obvious were the inclinations of two syndicated columnists, John Hanchette of the Gannett News Service (January 2, 1999) and Terry Mattingly of the Scripps-Howard chain (December 30, 1998), one of whom told me he had been at the prayer breakfast and left with serious doubts about the occasion, and the other having done a previous piece critical of Clinton. For all their "friendly" predispositions, the articles were "fair play." Hanchette accurately characterized the Declaration and its supporters, quoting four of the Declaration's points and its interpretive essays (Elshtain, Stackhouse), and from the interview with the writer, alluding to the fact that "many of the signers were self-declared proponents of Clinton's policies and from recognized bastions of liberal support," citing from the book's Preface that it was "troubled by both the high-profile religious pleas to 'forgive and forget' and by the war cries of the Religious Right." Hanchette also quotes from Nicholas Wolterstorff's essay critical of the Declaration. Mattingly did a shorter piece but caught the drift of both the Declaration and the book, quoting from the former and a key paragraph from Elshtain's chapter, and a memorable Conversation 1 comment of Hauerwas that "the question before Christians is not whether Bill Clinton should be impeached, but why he is not excommunicated." Mattingly did editorialize, observing that "perhaps Clinton represents today's Christian mainstream" with its promotion of religion as therapeutics and the giver of personal "meaning" rather than doctrine and truth-telling.

Jerry Filteau of the Catholic News Service did a thoughtful

piece (January 8, 1999) after retrieving the book from the give-away table where it had been placed by the Service's book reviewer, who had judged it inconsequential. He stressed the invitation-to-dialogue aspect of the Declaration, the web site, and the book, that "sparked a scholarly interfaith discussion on public morality . . . ," noting the Roman Catholic pro and con essays of Lamb of Boston College and Buckley of Georgetown. He gave attention, as well, to the critique of the prayer breakfast and how the Declaration came to be.

In the category of fair play fall various regional debates with both sides represented. Receiving most attention was an Elshtain-Wogaman exchange that took place February 1, 1999, at Fourth Presbyterian Church, Chicago, with attendant tapings for Ted Koppel's *Nightline* of February 4, 1999. That same night a parallel fair-minded debate involving Jewett and Snodgrass and critics took place at Wheaton College. For the ensuing months comparable exchanges between Declaration signers and critics occurred around the country, the last in the cycle being a March event at Old South Church, Boston. Representative of these less-well-known pro and con events were a PBS radio talk show and call-in program in Jackson, Mississippi (January 28, 1999), and *Detroit News* religion writer's George Bullard "Michiganians Take Sides on Clinton and Religion" (January 9, 1999).

Where to put "The O'Reilly Factor" show that interviewed Robert Jewett on Fox cable news channel? The host, O'Reilly, had been a consistent Clinton critic, but the producer warned potential interviewees that he had an "edge" and therefore not to expect coddling. (The producer went through other candidates, including the writer, before Jewett was signed on.) The interview itself was cordial, but the focus was O'Reilly's — the prayer breakfast and its religious ambiguities. And how about the early CNN interview and call-in program with Professor Elshtain (November 1998)? The interviewer was fair-minded but the callers were consistently hostile. Another hospitable venue was a two-hour talk program on Chicago's WGN with Jewett, Snodgrass, and Browning, later re-aired on C-Span.

Foul?

A foul ball is one hit by a batter outside the lines of play. What would that look like in media reportage? It would be an account that does not stay inside the lines of the event's givens and/or the information supplied to the reporter by the accountant. A foul by someone who could have hit a home run — someone on your own team — is a disappointment. Here is a sample of each in the unpredictable media world in which Declaration signers found themselves.

Peter Steinfels of *The New York Times* expressed interest in *Judgment Day at the White House,* inquiring by phone about the history, purpose, and points of the Declaration, about the rationale for the book and what those in the book defending the Declaration were trying to say. And, by the way, did you know about the volume by W. Philip Wogaman, the pastor of the congregation the president attends, who took a different view? Yes.

The article appeared a few days later in *The New York Times* (January 8, 1999). With an accompanying picture of Dr. Wogaman, it begins by referring to the appearance of two contrasting books, then cites and describes *From the Eye of the Storm.* Note is taken that the author is pastor to the president and also "for 26 years a professor of Christian ethics whose books on the topic are used as standard texts in Protestant seminaries around the country." Quotes are given from the volume, and its refrain is cited: "social discipline" is necessary and the president's behavior is not to be condoned, but "law and discipline . . . must be in the service of love and compassion." Noted is the juxtaposition by Wogaman of the prayer breakfast and the release of Starr's report as indicating "moral acts of repentance and forgiveness" vs. "judgment and condemnation."

And *Judgment Day at the White House*? Steinfels opens his comments with the observation that a "large number" of its essayists "obviously prefer the bluntness of the Starr report to the sentiment of the prayer breakfast." But the editorializing does segue to a mention of its leading themes — the manipulation of religion for political purposes, and the inseparability of personal and public morality with due recognition that the Declaration supporters "do not come from the religious right but largely from mainline Protestantism." For all that, Steinfels opines that many essays turn out to be "more than slightly high and mighty," their substantial arguments "weakened by their tight focus on Mr. Clinton." And style-wise, Wogaman "wins the face-off."

What are these "substantial arguments"? We do not find out. The only citations from the book are from one of the six essays *critical* of the Declaration. Nicholas Wolterstorff is quoted about his "amazement at the declaration's worry 'that the president might escape without punishment,'" and that "He has been placed in our model global equivalent of the stocks of a New England town . . . humiliated . . . to a degree beyond humiliation ever wreaked on another President." Wolterstorff, Steinfels says, "finds himself deeply troubled by the deliberate shaming — and by the declaration's silence about the moral questions it raises." So much for the *The New York Times* story on the "substance" of *Judgment Day at the White House*.

Can we expect more from our avowedly religious critics? We turn to Richard McBrien and his column, "Essays in Theology."[1]

---

1. Father McBrien is a long-time friend of the writer. We served together in the early years of Ph.D. programs of the Joint Graduate Faculty of Boston College and Andover Newton Theological School.

In the week of February 1, 1999, his "Politics and Morality: the Clinton Case" reviewed the Declaration and referred to the book, a piece appearing in fourteen Roman Catholic newspapers. Father McBrien teaches theology at Notre Dame and appears often on national television and in print media commenting on Roman Catholic aspects of current issues.

McBrien begins his essay by describing the Declaration signers as "drawn overwhelmingly from the conservative and evangelical wings of American Protestantism." He observes that only a handful of Roman Catholics appear and they too "tend to be as conservative as their Protestant counterparts." While he would not have signed the Declaration, he does credit it with protesting the apparent manipulation of religion and agrees that forgiveness does not relieve the president of acts of amendment. In the end, however, the Declaration fails for it "seems to allow politics to interfere with moral analysis," ignoring the fact that the president has "accepted moral responsibility for his behavior." Further, he "refused to admit that he committed perjury . . . or that he obstructed justice," a judgment made not by God but by "the Special Prosecutor and his political opponents."

The final half of the column focuses on matters of sex, denied by "political foes" as central but in fact the sub rosa issue for many, including "religious critics — Jerry Falwell, Pat Robertson and the Christian Coalition" — with whom Declaration signers are linked for "there is more than a hint" of the same in it. Fr. McBrien asks if the signers would apply the same standards to the critics of the president as they have to Mr. Clinton, observing that "perhaps Catholics are less prone than the many Protestants who drafted and signed this Declaration to render judgment about the sexually immoral conduct of others. . . ."

All the foregoing is about the Declaration. How about the book? Its contents are cited twice. However, each time the comments about it are from an essay by one of the Declaration's critics, Nicholas Wolterstorff. He is cited for not signing, and for alluding to the hypocrisy of Henry Hyde and his own self-defined "youthful indiscretion."

How is all of the above not a long loping foul ball over the left field fence? Here is the way its flight may be tracked: The signers of the Declaration are *not* "drawn overwhelmingly from conservative and evangelical wings of American Protestantism." As an actual scrutiny of the signatories indicates, and as other media accounts rightly report, the preponderance of supporters of the Declaration and all the Declaration interpreters in *Judgment Day at the White House* are from mainline or ecumenical (not evangelical) institutions, and many are political liberals. Further, to link the Declaration to "Jerry Falwell, Pat Robertson and the Christian Coalition" is a misreading not only of the Declaration's main issues and constituency, but also as preoccupied with issues of sexuality. Regarding *Judgment Day at the White House*, Fr. McBrien, unlike Steinfels, fails to credit it with inviting critics into the dialogue in the interest of civil conversation, but like Steinfels, draws only on the comments of Declaration critic Wolterstorff. Interestingly in this case, it is the politics of the issue to which the column refers, not the theological questions raised by Wolterstorff and throughout the volume by its other authors. How is the call on this "Essay in Theology" not . . . "foul ball"?

The Christian Century

Of interest to those of us who have always looked to *The Christian Century* as the organ of mainstream Christian commentary and reportage was the manner in which the presidential crisis was handled, and how the Declaration and the book were treated. (*Judgment Day at the White House* authors and Declaration signers Max Stackhouse, Don Browning, Stanley Hauerwas, Robert

Jewett, and the writer have been frequent authors of articles and reviews in the *Century*, Stackhouse being an editor at large. Declaration signers included columnist L. Gregory Jones and regular *Christian Century* contributors Mark Heim, Paul Achtemeier, Ellen Charry, and John Reumann.)

Then editor James Wall weighed into the controversy with a sharply worded "Unrepentant and Unforgiven" in the August 26–September 2, 1998, issue, bewailing "Clinton's Missed Opportunity" of public confession in his speech of August 17, 1998, and calling his "deception" and conduct "reprehensible."[2] An October 7, 1998, piece again found his "conduct . . . appalling and indefensible." But a new note appeared on that date. Wall wonders, was Ken Starr's work "really a service to the nation?" He answers, "likely, no." Further, politics is about "addressing issues of the common life" and "we would be wise to exempt politicians' private lives from the publicity of the public sphere."[3]

Shortly afterwards came another piece, this time done against the backdrop of the Clinton prayer breakfast of September 11. Editor Wall, who was at the breakfast, wrote on October 14 in an article entitled "There But for the Grace of God" that "Bill Clinton's remarks there more than made up for his less-than-contrite confession on the night of his grand jury appearance."[4] Editor Wall also strikes out at the "moralistic and angry voices by Clinton's enemies" and judges that "the religious and secular right is trying to create a clamor of moralistic judgment against Clinton . . . ," declaring that "Starr's "Christian fundamentalist background gives him the single-minded passion of a

2. James M. Wall, "Unrepentant, Unforgiven," *The Christian Century* 115, no. 23 (August 26–September 2, 1998): 771.

3. James M. Wall, "Appalling Behavior," *The Christian Century* 115, no. 26 (October 7, 1998): 801.

4. James M. Wall, "There But for the Grace of God," *The Christian Century* 115, no. 27 (October 14, 1998): 922.

zealot determined to eradicate evil and punish wrongdoers."
We've come a long way from August 26 to October 14.

Editor Wall gets specific about some moralists on December
9. They turn out to be the signers of the Declaration. In "Come
on Down," he invites this self-righteous crowd to come on down
the aisle and repent with the rest of the sinners who have made
that trip. Join Bill Clinton instead of keeping him "in the sinners' box" while you "carry on that discussion" about what repentance means. And the repentant president, there at the rail,
"speaks one more time: 'Come on down, we will wait.' "[5]

Wall had one more salvo on the subject, "Wild Children," on
January 27, 1999, appealing for an end to the "unfairness" of the
charges brought by Kenneth Starr and also the unkind cuts of
James Carville, each perpetuating the "cycle of seeking revenge."
For all that, the "case of Henry Hyde," his vendetta and hypocrisy, was the subject of much of the article. Its conclusion is a la-
ment: like the school playground fight among children, ven-
geance is the order of the day, and "there are no teachers around
to step in and halt the carnage. And that just isn't fair."[6]

In a similar defense of the president, *The Christian Century*
published an article by Walter Wink, "Apology in Statecraft: Excuse Me!" Drawing on his New Testament studies, Wink argued
that Jesus "does not wait on sinners to repent. . . . You were enemies and yet God accepts you! There is nothing you must do to
earn this. You need only to accept it. So should we forgive
Clinton? God has already done so. . . . If we consider ourselves
more just than God, I suppose we can refuse to forgive him."[7]

5. James M. Wall, "Come on Down!" *The Christian Century* 115, no. 34
(December 9, 1998): 1171.

6. James M. Wall, "Wild Children," *The Christian Century* 116, no. 3 (January 27, 1999).

7. Walter Wink, "Excuse Me!" *The Christian Century* 115, no. 28 (October
21, 1998): 956.

Besides, Clinton has been punished enough, so let's forgive him and "get on with the business of state."

The articles of Wall and Wink did not pass without critical response. Such came in letters to the editor from some of the Declaration signers. Don Browning wrote, "James Wall's two recent editorials for the most part miss the point on the crisis surrounding Bill Clinton." Browning faults Wall for focusing on sexual misconduct to the exclusion of the substantial charges of perjury, obstruction of justice, and abuse of power, and for wanting to end the impeachment process before some judgment is rendered. Signer Edward Ericson of Calvin College missed the editor's "fair engagement" with the Declaration. He observes that Wall dismisses it with "faint scorn," and the sniffing of "self-righteousness," falling into a "bizarre" characterization of the president as the "nation's senior pastor," ironically confirming the Declaration's protest of the use of religion for political purposes. Why not let his penitence appear in public form, taking the legal consequences of lies under oath? The writer added his own letter to the editor to the exchange, drawing on Bonhoeffer's paradox in response to the Wink article: grace is free but not cheap, as in the reparations given to Japanese-Americans as a sign of the seriousness of the country's act of repentance, so cited by Wink himself. Both Wall and Wink had their supporters in the Letters columns.

Christian Century attention to 1998-99 presidential doings was rounded out by a cover story review of both *Judgment Day at the White House* and Wogaman's *From the Eye of the Storm* by the new executive editor, David Heim.[8] It breathed a different

8. David Heim, "Judging Clinton: The Religious Debate," *The Christian Century* 116, no. 8 (March 10, 1999): 278-81. James Wall retired from the editorship and was replaced by John Buchanan, pastor of Fourth Presbyterian Church, Chicago. Under a different arrangement, the newly created post of "executive editor" assumed the primary day-to-day editorial responsibilities.

spirit than earlier editorial pieces, although Heim continued the "no impeachment" position of Wall. He carefully laid out Wogaman's main points: "the essence of morality is love, not law"; while Clinton's conduct had to be criticized, this is a moment for "healing, reconciliation and restoration . . . compassion not judgment"; the prayer breakfast contrition was a "deeply religious moment"; Clinton's affair, "while reprehensible, was essentially private"; the partisanship, zealotry, and self-righteousness of the president's critics are part of the picture as well. While acknowledging some validity to the "practical judgments" (such as removal of an elected president on these grounds being a dangerous precedent, public exposure being a penalty in itself), Heim finds "as a tool of analysis, Wogaman's ethic of non-judgmental love [to be] a rather flimsy instrument." He suspects Wogaman would not follow out its logic in other circumstances such as a Watergate or a case of racial discrimination, where judgment cannot be canceled by forgiveness and "reconciliation can take place only after justice has been served." Heim is also troubled by the "rhetoric of the argument," which judges that calls for public scrutiny of Clinton or further penalties are "loveless and unforgiving." He warns of a "danger for mainline churches" in the argument, as it reflects a history of preoccupation with social issues and neglect of personal morality, one that fails to recognize the data now available that "private issues of marriage and sexuality have very public ramifications. . . ."

And *Judgment Day* . . . ? Heim comments on the Declaration and two of its supporting essays, with passing reference to one of the six Declaration critics. He cites the questions raised by the Declaration about the political use of the prayer breakfast and its assertion of the inseparability of personal morality and the public order. He commends its call for further debate and the effort of the book to facilitate such by including six critical essays. He agrees with the proponents of the Declaration that appeals to Christian forgiveness do not eliminate the need to consider the charges and to take up things: "Wogaman does not say anything about the egregious ways Clinton betrayed trust, exploited an employee, tarnished public discourse, and perhaps broke the law." However, there are problems, especially so with "some of the essayists" who have not sorted out the "many dimensions of the case." Further, both the Declaration and the book show a "remarkable deficiency" in their inattention to Starr's politically motivated and zealous investigation, so cited by Declaration critic Nicholas Wolterstorff.

Heim concentrates his Declaration criticism on those who have appeared throughout the controversy in high-profile debates and interviews, Jean Bethke Elshtain and Robert Jewett. Elshtain's contention that "the Oval Office is not enveloped within a private *cordon sanitaire*," personal behavior in this case moving "into the public domain in every possible scale — ethical, legal and political," leaves Heim with "nagging questions." While private and public matters are not to be "totally separated," they must be "distinguished in some way," or else the most rudimentary family problem becomes fair game for public rebuke. Further, most Americans do hold the president accountable, but question impeachment and removal as the proper penalties. And he wonders why she takes a moralistic view of the matter when her writings have always recognized the moral ambiguities of political life.

Heim credits Jewett with a "shrewd analysis of Clinton's speech" at the prayer breakfast and a realism about the abuse of religion for political purposes, but argues that such a religious indictment and the questioning of the completeness of repentance are not germane to the question of impeachment and removal from office, matters based on the "constitutional significance of his deeds." Heim wonders if the linkage by Jewett and the Declaration signers of the two suggests that impeachment and removal are thought by them to be the outworking of genuine contrition. He calls again on Wolterstorff who argues that Clinton was willing to accept punishment, but "the issue for him was the level of punishment." In short, the issues of repentance and impeachment cannot be conflated. For all that, Heim appreciates the point made by the Declaration and its supporters that "repentance is a matter not of saying a few opportune words but of taking up practical tasks that can take years, perhaps a lifetime, to realize."

Here is a conversation worth having. The *Christian Century* executive editor has given fair-minded attention to the Declaration and two of its most important interpreters. He acknowledges the importance of some of the leading themes of the Declaration and its companion volume: the inseparability, at least to some extent, of personal and public morality; the danger of using professions of repentance and faith as a means to political ends; the need to demonstrate repentance in deed as well as to declare it in word; the inadequacy of an ethical analysis that juxtaposes love to law, accompanied in Clinton supporters by accusations of lovelessness in those who accent law. But a rejoinder is in order on some matters.

While the fault lies as much with those of us who signed the Declaration and wrote about it, it is also true that Heim has confused the two conversations discussed in an earlier chapter. One is about fundamental questions of faith addressed to Clinton and his religious supporters, indeed having political consequences because matters spiritual and secular are inseparable. The other is about fundamental questions of governance which are to be adjudicated on their own merits, for spiritual and political matters while inseparable are also distinguishable.[9] The

---

9. A point made in the writer's chapter of *Judgment Day at the White House* (Grand Rapids: Eerdmans, 1999), pp. 99-107.

Declaration and book are, preeminently, a voice in the first conversation. The most obvious example of that is the assertion in point 6 of the Declaration of the disagreement among signers about both impeachment and resignation, and the comparable diversity of views in the chapters of those supporting the Declaration. Distinguishability does not preclude serious political consequences, and that precisely on the religious grounds upon which the conversation is conducted. Here the theological struggle with the meaning of Christian repentance is germane. Heim rightly affirms the role of "reparation — concrete, practical reparation" in genuine repentance. Considering the widespread and continuing effects of Clinton's conduct, resignation would indeed have been a responsible act of penitence in the interest of the public weal.[10] That kind of serious political consequence taken *at the penitent's initiative* coheres with the Declaration's intentions. Thus the point is not, as Heim intimates, that the call for repentance constitutes the criterion *for others* to remove the president from office. The latter is determined by constitutional standards, not religious ones. To merge the two is to confuse the conversations.

Professor Elshtain is well able to defend her theses in *Judgment Day at the White House*, and does so in a brilliant review of Wogaman's *From the Eye of the Storm* and an interesting volume by Gordon MacDonald, whose own journey as a pastor into and back from infidelity prompted his invitation to be one of Clinton's counselors. Here, however, two specifics need to be mentioned. Does her stress on the moral accountability of a president open the door to the investigation of any delinquencies in the Pennsylvania Avenue household or any compromised political actions? Not if the Declaration she helped draft is read carefully, for it addresses just that issue. Point 4 asserts that per-

10. *Judgment Day at the White House*, p. 102.

fection is not expected and that "morally problematic actions" are, to use Heim's phrase, "the stuff of politics." However, the Declaration asserts that "there is a reasonable threshold of behavior beneath which our public leaders should not fall. . . ." To charge that her contention (that the personal and the political are inextricable) invites public investigation of any and all mischievousness is, simply, to take no account of the "threshold" premise.

And a final observation. The suggestion that the Declaration points to impeachment and removal from office as the required outcome of the episode has no basis in the text. Neither can it be found in the essays of Elshtain and Jewett or any of the other *Judgment Day* interpreters of the Declaration. Here the distinction between the two conversations is important, as well as the related differences between actions taken by a penitent and those imposed against the penitent's will. The making of a Declaration and the writing of a book in the midst of an investigatory procedure are evidence that the signers and supporting authors are participating *also* in Conversation 2 with its involvement in impeachment and removal issues, although with differing views on those subjects. While there is no entailment of specific penalties, their assertion of threshold personal morality for the nation's highest office supports the right to investigate serious evidence of the breach of presidential conduct. That members of the president's own party defending him from impeachment and removal in those venues insistently pressed for a strong censure of his personal behavior supports the Declaration's assertion of public accountability for "reprehensible" personal behavior. The promotion of the censure resolution by those pleading for the separation of private and public behavior in judging the president moves us to the ironies with which this crisis is replete.

Chapter 4

Ironies

I rony is the "incongruity between what might be expected and what actually occurs."[1] Reinhold Niebuhr had a special eye for such juxtapositions, linking them to the sin of pride that masks our pretensions and showing how they play out in the political arena.[2] He took special account of the incongruities of the "righteous." The nation or political movement or religious constituency that prides itself on being the instrument of rectitude can readily see the sins in the foes of justice, freedom, and peace, but not in its champions. The irony is compounded when the contradiction between profession and practice itself is joined to a self-righteous fury.

The ironies Niebuhr discovered in our American history continued in the end-century presidential crisis. As judgment

1. William Morris, ed., *The American Heritage Dictionary of the English Language* (Boston: American Heritage Publishing Co. and Houghton Mifflin Co., 1973), p. 692.

2. So Reinhold Niebuhr, *The Irony of American History* (New York: Macmillan, 1982). He also explored such juxtapositions in relation to humor as in "Humor and Faith," *Discerning the Signs of the Times* (New York: Charles Scribner's Sons, 1946), pp. 111-31.

begins with the "household of God," the focus here is on those who, like myself, have been associated with movements that tout their advocacy for the outcast, the poor, and the disenfranchised. While there is plenty of evidence of similar lack of congruence in the ranks of the Religious Right — righteous indignation smokescreening political agendas, prurience portrayed as "the rule of law," etc. — let each look to its own.

Role Reversal

Passing allusion was made earlier to the unforeseen in our encounters with the media. We linger here on a pattern of irony in newspapers known for their professions of justice and their reputation for publishing "all the news that's fit to print." For social activists this number has always included *The New York Times,* *The Washington Post,* and the *Boston Globe.* Dissenters in this presidential crisis remembered the attention given by them to similar issues in the presidential crisis a quarter of a century earlier. Thus *The Washington Post* exposed the abuse of Nixonian power and risked the wrath of the political establishment in both its editorial courage and reportorial daring. On matters comparable to the present issues, the *Post*'s religion writer was the first to air the concerns of religious leaders about "White House religion" and "White House ethics," as earlier noted.[3]

And on the present watch for presidential malfeasance and criticism by religious leaders of "White House religion" and "White House ethics"? On December 26, 1998, Washington attention *was* drawn to the subject in a prominent article on the Declaration:

3. Marjorie Heyer, "Clerics View Watergate Differently," May 18, 1973, B22.

The declaration asserts that private and public morality cannot be separated, as the White House has spun the issue in the national debate. The declaration also protested Mr. Clinton's apparent manipulation of clergy at his nationally televised prayer breakfast on September 13. . . .[4]

This report appeared, however, not in *The Washington Post* but in *The Washington Times*. Nothing about the Declaration was ever printed in the former, except in an ad placed by its signatories and supporters. (The ad, carefully scheduled by its purchasers for the closing days of the House debate, was lost by the newspaper. It was later printed during the Senate hearings.) If religious dissent about "White House religion" and "White House ethics" this time around was to be heard in the pages of Washington's self-appointed social conscience, it had to be at a price.

And *The New York Times?* Yes, the Declaration and *Judgment Day at the White House* did receive attention in the aforementioned piece by Peter Steinfels. How they received it is another matter. As noted, the dissent was cited in a puff piece on the *assenting* pastor of the president, with no discussion of the substance of the book or Declaration, except to quote from a Declaration critic. Would the *Times* print a "letter to the editor" laying out the Declaration issues? One from dissenting Democrats taking issue with the reporting and editorial refrain that the affair was essentially a Republican vendetta against the president? Many tries were made, but no letter ever appeared. Was the Declaration news not "fit to print"? Not entirely, for it did make its way to page A6 of the January 12, 1999, issue, once again, as with the *Post*, as an advertisement sponsored by its supporters.

4. Larry Witham, "Ethicists Who Supported Clinton Fault His Moral Posture," *The Washington Times*, December 26, 1998, A4.

And the writer's hometown paper, the *Boston Globe*? Surely, its editors had seen reports of the Declaration in national media, on network programs, and cited in congressional hearings. How could it fail to see the newsworthy signatures from Boston College faculty and other schools in the region? With its reputation for going against the stream, how could it miss this voice of dissent?

A Boston story did finally appear, one day following the February 4, 1999, White House prayer breakfast. The article, "Clinton's 'Cheap Forgiveness' Upsets Local Religious Scholars," commented on the president's remarkable comparison of his impeachment problems to another world figure's long internment: "If Nelson Mandela can walk away from 28 years of oppression in a little prison cell, we can walk away from whatever is bothering us." Stephen Pope, professor at Boston College, is also quoted commenting on the self-serving overtones heard in both prayer breakfasts:

> "The president has tried to use Christian ministers and Christian churches as a way to gain cheap forgiveness," said Stephen J. Pope, director of undergraduate studies at Boston College. "The cheap forgiveness is cheap because it doesn't really ask him to pay a price for what he has done."

The article went on to describe the Declaration and *Judgment Day at the White House*, listing and quoting other area signers. Thus Boston readers did learn of dissenting voices. But not from the *Boston Globe*. The article appeared on page 2 of the *Boston Herald*, seen by the *Globe* as its biased right-wing competitor. As with the *Globe*'s owner, *The New York Times*, no letter to the editor, sent by Declaration participants to the *Globe* in protest of the newspaper's reporting, was printed. Dissent on this issue, as far as this voice of liberalism was concerned, would be "banned in Boston."

Guilt by Association

Earlier mention was made of the McCarthyism of the 1950s, which charged political liberals with being either "comsymps" (communist sympathizers) or outright communists. Especially so when they defended free speech and voices of dissent.[5] The responding argument was: judge our views on their merits, not by scurrilous linkages with movements we too oppose . . . "guilt by association." The latter came to be recognized for what it was, the technique of a demagogic McCarthyism.

Guilt by association, however, has a thousand lives. At the end of the century it appeared again. This time it was used to discredit presidential critics. "Hasn't Senator Trent Lott been an apologist for the heirs of the infamous White Citizens' Council of Mississippi?[6] Didn't Representative Henry Hyde lead the fight for the pro-life forces? Wasn't Representative Bob Barr affiliated with racist movements in his state?" The citation of associations of the enemy, purported or proven, effectively diverted attention from the issue at hand in 1999 as it did 50 years ago.

The *irony* is that the charge of consorting with the disreputable is deployed by my own political kin who suffered from this tactic a half century ago, and who rightly mounted the counter-charge of "guilt by association." And the same self-righteous fury of the 1950s was apparent in those who used the tactic this time around. But we can hope that the "guilt by association" argument of the 1990s will prove, in time, to be as bogus as it was in the 1950s. Yet the incongruity between what might be ex-

5. Thus President Hutchins of the University of Chicago in 1950 resisted the "Broyles Bills" in the Illinois legislature that would have required a loyalty oath of university teachers. The writer went to the state capitol along with others in the noncommunist Americans for Democratic Action to protest the bill.

6. John Kifner, "Lott, and the Shadow of a Pro-White Group," *The New York Times*, January 14, 1999, A9.

pected from liberals burned by the unfairness they charged their opponents with in another day, and their recourse to the same ploy in their own time, is one more "irony of American history."

The Separation of Private and Public

If there was any one refrain in the defense of President Clinton's behavior during the crisis, it was the demand to respect the private space of a citizen, especially so the holder of the highest office in the land. "Don't meddle in our personal lives! It's between the president and his family, and none of your business!"

Throughout the debate, Declaration signers contended for the opposite view: the personal and the public cannot be so separated. The inner life of a leader is the "crucible" in which a political will is formed, as Garry Wills expressed it. And now some of the president's close former associates make the same case.[7]

Ironically, while insisting on the separation of private and public life, many defenders of the president fought hard for a censure vote in the Congress, and that for his *personal* behavior. To this day, Democrats fault the Republican majority for preventing this action in both the House and the Senate. How is this the separation of the private from the public so passionately espoused by the same people? The highest legislative body in the land, and the most powerful political forum in the world, is asked to take a formal vote on the personal conduct of an American president. The proposed text, and the rhetoric supporting it, speak of this behavior as "reprehensible." Thus the incongruity of the defenders of separation becoming the ardent advocates of a measure to unite them.

7. So George Stephanopolis in *All Too Human: A Political Education* (Boston: Little, Brown, 1999).

Sexual Misconduct

"Liberation!" came to be a watchword for many of us in the 1970s.[8] The oppressed will no longer take things lying down. Women mounted their own "freedom revolution" in the wake of, and often in conjunction with, other marginalized groups. One of the achievements of their protest movement was the institution of sexual harassment laws. The abuse of women in the workplace would no longer be tolerated. Powerful men who used their status to prey sexually on their female employees would now be held accountable for their actions. Loss of their jobs was not the least of the penalty to be paid. In the struggle, "the personal *is* the political" became a feminist watchword.

An irony of current American history is the position on the presidential crisis taken by leading feminist exponents of liberation, indeed those who helped to raise public awareness about sexual misconduct in the workplace. "What's the big deal?" asks Betty Friedan. So the vigorous support of a president charged in court with sexual harassment, and later settling the suit out of court for a large sum of money. So the attack by the same on critics who sought to hold him accountable for his sexual advances toward a workplace intern. How are the defense and attack not incongruous with the claim that "the personal is the political"?

Feminist support of Clinton — and the silence of other North American advocates of liberation — is related to their focus on structural issues of oppression. Clinton is seen as a professed advocate of justice in domestic issues and peace in inter-

8. Gabriel Fackre, *Liberation in Middle America* (Philadelphia: Pilgrim Press, 1971), was my attempt to stretch the concept to include the working classes as well as the ethnic and gender constituencies who had adopted the *Kampfbegriff*. "Liberation and reconciliation" continues to be a theme in my *Christian Story* series (Grand Rapids: Eerdmans, 1978, 1984, 1988, 1996).

national affairs. But several incongruities present themselves.
(1) The president's credibility has been seriously weakened as a
result of the moral crisis, affecting in turn his capacity to exe-
cute the programs of domestic justice and international peace
that he espouses. The linkage disavowed in practice or theory
has a way of reasserting itself. (2) Questions must be asked
about the extent to which the president's performance lives up
to the credit given him on matters of justice and peace. Critics
Andrew Sullivan and Christopher Hitchens, who link the personal and public Clinton, call him sharply to account on the
very practice of "liberation" in policy decisions.[9] Surely Jesse
Jackson, who defended Clinton during the presidential crisis,
cannot help but wonder about the response he received from the
administration to Jackson's own dramatic peace initiative in
Kosovo.

And ironies appear along yet another liberation front line.
"Ageism" is regularly linked with sexism, racism, and other op-
pressive isms. Under each is a vulnerable segment of American
society. Forbidden is the caricature and put-downs long associated with the ism. What then do we make of Maureen Dowd's
column on some "elder" statespersons? Flailing "Peter and Dan
and Tom and Tim and Cokie" for their talk of congressional proceedings as "moving, solemn . . . momentous, dead serious and
bold," she declaims, "If I were describing the occasion . . . I
would use the word *old*. I might use the word *dead*. . . . Call it
the revenge of the Grumpy Old Men. . . ."[10] While "Senator
Thurmond, 96 . . . Robert Byrd, 81, and Chief Justice

9. Christopher Hitchens, "It's Not the Sin, It's the Cynicism," *Vanity Fair*
(December 1998): 138-46. Hitchens further develops his critique "From the
Left" in *No One Left to Lie To: The Triangulations of William Jefferson Clinton*
(New York: Verso Books, 1999).

10. Maureen Dowd, "Avid Ovid Readers," Op-Ed, *The New York Times*,
January 10, 1999, Section 4, 21.

Rehnquist, 74," get taken to task for their age, her choicest scorn is reserved for "Henry Hyde lumbering across the marbled halls . . . leading that pack of gray-haired, gray-faced, gray-suited and gray-spirited fogies" that turn out to be "self-appointed Torquemadas [who] looked more like gouty Florida retirees hurrying to get to the early-bird buffet." Here is a virulent ageism, as out of bounds as partner racism, sexism, and anti-Semitism would be in the pages of *The New York Times*. So much for outrage over today's isms. Perhaps the final irony is the Pulitzer prize given to Dowd for her columns on the presidential crisis.

Word and Deed

How often church social activists assert the importance of the *deed* in making a Christian witness. How much the reduction of faith to its interiorities is bewailed. How despised those who settle for pious words rather than action, especially sacrificial action. In the 1970s when "evangelism!" became the cry ("Key 73" in the United States), mainline churches reproved the pietists who launched crusades to save souls but ignored the concern to change society. The writer was among those who wrote books and took part in movements of "word in deed" evangelization, critical of standard-brand evangelical mission that appeared to settle for "word" and ignored the companion "deed" of Acts 2–4.[11]

Notable in the defense of President Clinton's repentance by fellow-mainliners and fellow-political liberals is the refrain, "Why don't you take him at his word! He said he's sorry . . . over and over again. What more do you want?" To this is added by the more theologically oriented: "Grace is free! Christ took care

11. Developed in *Do and Tell* (Grand Rapids: Eerdmans, 1973) and *Word in Deed* (Grand Rapids: Eerdmans, 1975).

of our sins. Trust the divine forgiveness. Don't make conditions for God's unconditional love!"[12]

The ardent support of Clinton by activists who both earlier and also now insist on the cruciality of action to authenticate faith is a major irony. The incongruity may be accounted for by Clinton's espousal of a political agenda that coheres with a justice agenda. To secure him against his conservative foes, we must accept his profession of repentance at its face value and allow him to go forward with the good programs for which he stands. The means toward that end is a theology that counts the word of confession as the sufficient sign of repentance.

There are two issues here. The first is *theological*. Does verbal confession constitute repentance? "No," says a long tradition in the church. It entails not only "confession of the mouth," but also "contrition of the heart" and "satisfaction" by hands and feet. The first two require the public evidence of the third. Settling for the word alone short-circuits the fullness of repentance. We shall explore the theology of repentance further in the next chapter.

The second issue is *logical*. How can one insist that doing the deed is essential and vigorously condemn those who "talk the talk but don't walk the walk," yet then settle in the presidential crisis for words alone? And then condemn those who press for the authenticating deed? Here is "an incongruity between what is expected and what occurs."

The Political Mission of the Mainline

How eager many of us in the mainline churches have been to be heard by the culture of our day. Not to be ushered off to private

12. As in Walter Wink, "Excuse Me!" *The Christian Century* 115, no. 28 (October 21, 1998): 956-58.

quarters where mannerly religion can carry out its delimited role of "hatching, matching, and dispatching" (baptism, marriage, and burial). We say "No!" to this marginalization by a secular society with its Enlightenment stratagems. Our charge is to enter boldly the public square . . . to do "public theology"! We cannot forget that we did just that in the halcyon days of the civil rights struggle, making a difference in public policy. Hasn't the Religious Right fooled everyone by leaving its apolitical pietism for a raucous political fundamentalism, having (another irony!) learned it from the Martin Luther King, Jr., that we followed into that earlier fray?[13]

But for many years secular society has paid little attention to our church resolutions on current affairs, and our current social action agendas and agencies. What then do we make of the sudden attention given to a rump group of religionists whose indignations are quoted in congressional hearings? Or of its protest book, much reviewed in the popular media?

The irony here is that the much coveted hearing the mainline gets in the public square is not prompted by the determinedly public posture of its official agencies, but by the focus on personal issues by some of its contrarian cohorts. That the personal is inseparable from the political is something that many standard-brand social activists have yet to learn, if not from other Christians, then perhaps from the generation of feminists who coined the phrase.

13. Jerry Falwell paid tribute to Martin Luther King, Jr., for so inspiring him. See Frances Fitgerald, "A Disciplined, Charging Army," *The New Yorker*, May 18, 1981, pp. 60-63, 113-14.

Assyrian Rods

Scripture speaks of God's unpredictabilities. Thus the Lord of history can use the enemies of Israel to make a point. The foreign king, Nebuchadnezzar, is the divine choice to be the "rod of God's anger" in reproving the chosen people. The lessons of Hebrew history may have their counterpart in end-century American history — at least for those of us who associate the divine purposes with the social agenda of the mainline churches, one often parallel to the programs of the Democratic party and political left-of-center policies.

One presidential crisis irony for the latter is the possibility that the Republican party, our political "enemy," may be the Assyrian rod. Who now speaks a good word for the personal virtues? The inextricability of the private and the public? Who bewails the "death of outrage"? Who risked public scorn and the loss of future elections for pressing the case for presidential accountability? Who marched to the beat of a different drummer than the sound of the popular polls? Why do Declaration signers and book essayists, long-critical of both the religious and secular right, find their work greeted with silence or contempt by their allies but welcomed by Christian radio and the Fox News channel? Of course, the answer is that we are striking notes that fit the agenda of the "enemy." Could it be that what we have considered to be the "children of darkness . . . are in this generation wiser than the children of light"? (Luke 16:8). Better still, lockstep church ideology — of the left or right — needs to be reminded ever and again of a "freedom in Christ" that takes its signals from the "One Word," rather than simplistically dividing the world up neatly into the Manichaean camps of "darkness" and "light."

Of particular pain were the frequent charges of our longtime allies — mainstream church activists, establishment ethicists, Democratic comrades — that we are dupes of our conservative foes. Never mind that the removal of the president would put in place a vice-president committed to the same policies, and give us a chance to move on from preoccupations that left little time for our common agenda, or left a weakened presidency in place to erode that agenda. Forget the six Republicans who on the Judiciary in another time of impeachment parted company with their colleagues to indict Nixon, in comparison with the uncritical fealty of Democrats to their president this time around.

Yet why this departure from their party's line by signatories and interpreters of the Declaration? It has to do with their understanding of theological integrity and biblical faithfulness. "Integrity" is the matter of wholeness, in this case the inclusivity of ethics that partners personal and public morality. When one or the other is neglected, integrity dies. The right is known for its reduction of ethics to the personal and the left for its reduction of ethics to the public issues. Biblical faithfulness is two freedoms — the freedom of God and the freedom of the believer. In the first case, God is free to pour out uncovenanted mercies on enemy nations. In the second, Christ calls the believer to be free enough to make unconventional alliances. This final Assyrian rod of irony points toward important lessons, theological and biblical, that have come from engagement with the presidential crisis. To these we now turn.

Chapter 5

Lessons

What can be learned from the presidential crisis? Its ironies and distinguishable conversations are lessons in themselves. But more, what learnings on fundamental matters of faith and life, the stuff of Conversation 1?[1]

Repentance

The presidential crisis prompted a wide-ranging discussion of repentance. The language and locations of Clinton's professions — before and with religious leaders and in relation to Christian congregations — makes repentance and its correlate, forgiveness, subjects in Conversation 1. Allusion has already been made to them.

Theological arguments were made by presidential protagonists along one of two lines: (1) "Christ died for our sins. The di-

---

1. For an earlier memo, see the writer's chapter, "Christian Doctrine and Presidential Decisions," *Judgment Day at the White House* (Grand Rapids: Eerdmans, 1999), pp. 99-110.

vine mercy takes away the divine judgment. Grace is free, no conditions are required, not even our repentance. If God forgives President Clinton, we must also." (2) "Repentance is needed before we can be forgiven. The president *has* repented. What more do you want?" Both these contentions are right in what they affirm, and wrong in what they deny.

The Reformation was a signal moment in Christian history, bringing to the fore "justification by grace through faith" so often obscured by "works-righteousness." Thus the watchwords, "grace alone, faith alone . . . Christ alone." In the life, death, and resurrection of Jesus Christ, God reconciled the world, centrally so on the cross where the consequences of our sin were removed by the vicarious suffering of the divine-human Person. Through the church's "means of grace," in trusting faith, we receive the merciful benefits of Christ's saving work. Where does repentance come into this account? In classical teaching it is always linked to "faith" and located at two places in the Christian's pilgrimage. The first is at the point of coming to personal faith, whether in the revolutionary moment of conversion or the evolutionary growth into faith through the church's nurture. (Traditions differ on the relation of "law" to "gospel" in the engendering of repentance and faith.) The second is constituted by acts of repentance that take place in the subsequent journey of faith, whether they be in the church's liturgies of confession — public or private — or in deep moments of self-awareness of our sin committed, then confessed. In both cases, repentance is inseparable from faith.

What does the word mean? It comes clear in these biblical usages. Christ declares, "The kingdom of God has come near; repent and believe the good news" (Mark 1:15 NRSV). Peter asserts, "Repent, and be baptized every one of you in the name of Jesus Christ so that your sins may be forgiven . . ." (Acts 2:38 NRSV). In both cases, "repent!" is a call for change in direction.

The Greek word, *metanoia*, which appears in these texts and many similar ones in the New Testament (with counterpart in the *subh* of the Old Testament),[2] means an *about-face*. More specifically, it is a turning *from* something — a freedom from enslavement. Commenting on the Acts description of the journey of conversion, New Testament scholar Charles Carlston remarks that "If any distinction is made between *metanoein* and *epistrephein* in the New Testament, it is that *metanoein* emphasizes more strongly the element of turning away from the old, *epistrephein* turning toward the new" (Acts 3:10, 26:20).[3] Repentance is a wrenching loose from old ways to a new Way, always by the grace of God. It can happen in the primal act of allegiance to Jesus Christ ("conversion"), or in subsequent returnings from deviancies large or small along the new *hodos* (path, way).

The metaphor of "turning from" is vividly illustrated by the story of the prodigal son. His profession of repentance, "Father, I have sinned against heaven and before you . . ." (Luke 15:21), was linked to his about-face. Turning here meant movement of the feet away from the "distant country" (Luke 15:13) and a travel homeward. Repentance, therefore, is a change of behavior as well as a change of heart, a redirection of the whole being that "walks the walk" as well as "talks the talk."

A classical tradition of repentance has formulated these biblical understandings of new direction as a threefold movement: contrition of the heart, confession of the mouth, and satisfaction by hands and feet.[4] The turning entailed in the act of repen-

---

2. See William Holladay, *The Root Subh in the Old Testament* (Leiden: Brill, 1958).

3. Charles Edwin Carlston, "Metanoia and Church Discipline" (unpublished Ph.D. dissertation, Harvard University, 1959).

4. See "Penance," *A Catholic Dictionary*, ed. Donald Atwater (New York: Macmillan, 1961), 376-77.

tance — in this case in practices of church confession on the Christian's journey of faith — cannot exclude any of these dimensions. The last movement — of the hands and feet — captures the physical re-turning of the prodigal. The only way he could receive the forgiving embrace of the father was to make the turn and take that foot journey home.

The father's move toward the son was the foundational turn of mercy. Without any knowledge of why the son was returning (could it be to get more money from the parent?), while the son yet was "still far off," the father rushed to meet and embrace him. The son did not have to prove himself worthy *first*. The parent's love was unmerited, unconditional. No good work was required. Considering the rigorous Semitic patriarchal standards of accountability, how can we explain the father's act? Where did the righteous anger and just judgment go?

The cross helps us to understand what transpired at the home end of that road. Indeed, the two stories interpret each other. On Calvary the mercy of God absorbs the wrath of God, as Luther put it. God takes into the divine heart all the consequences of our sin. In like manner, the loving father takes into his own being his judgment on the prodigal son. So the welcome of an unconditional *agape* awaits all of us prodigals, a mercy born of suffering love. Grace is free!

But it is not *cheap*. Costly grace means a receiving in kind at our own end of the painful turn at God's end. Such a receiving entails the responding movements of the heart, mouth, and feet. The contrite prodigal made both a confession of the mouth and an act of amendment, the turn homeward. We too only "come home" to the free unmerited mercy of another Father with a move of both heart and feet toward the offered embrace. In theological terms, the objective grace of God is met by our subjective repentant faith. The seed flowers only in fertile soil.

We are reminded ever and again of the place of faith/repentance on the Christian's journey in the liturgies of the church. So the "assurance of pardon" in a standard rite:

> Hearken now unto the comforting assurance of the grace of God, promised in the Gospel to all who repent and believe. . . . Unto as many of you . . . as truly repent of your sins, and believe in the Lord Jesus Christ, with full purpose of new obedience, I announce and declare by the authority and in the name of Christ, that your sins are forgiven, according to his promise in the Gospel.[5]

In sum, grace *is* free, the fruit of an unmerited divine act of mercy toward a rebel world. Those cited above who assert the same are right in what they affirm. Yet they are wrong in what they deny. Grace *is not* cheap, for it is "promised in the Gospel to all who repent and believe," an act of faith inextricable from repentance. So too those who assert the cruciality of repentance in receiving the forgiveness offered are right in what they affirm, yet wrong in what they deny. Again grace is not cheap, for the *full* act of repentance entails signs of "new obedience" that makes amends for harm done.

Freedom

"Freedom" is a familiar word in both secular and religious discourse. One of its meanings came forcefully home in the presidential crisis: Can we be sufficiently free *from* our usual human (in this case, political) loyalties to be free *for* something other than those standard commitments? Especially so when that

---

5. "Assurance of Pardon," *The Hymnal* (St. Louis, Mo.: Eden Publishing House, 1947), p. 5.

"other" has been associated with a long-time enemy? Some of the ironies earlier described bring these questions into the arena of theology. For Christians, freedom has to do with "freedom in Christ":

> For freedom Christ has set us free. Stand firm, therefore, and do not submit again to a yoke of slavery. (Galatians 5:1)

St. Paul speaks here to an early congregation about freedom from the *law*, trust in justification before God by grace through faith. In other times, freedom is about struggles against other bondages — race, class, sex, condition. Why not now, yet again this Galatian shout for freedom, this time liberation from ideological slavery? Christian freedom in this case would mean freedom from penultimate partisanships in order to be free for an ultimate loyalty.

Reinhold Niebuhr had something like this in mind when he spoke about relativizing predictable associations, challenging the conventional wisdom that one must be found on the *theological* right if one is on the *political* right, and vice versa. But, he asked, why cannot one move "politically to the left and theologically to the right"? He did just that. In a similar refusal to be put in a box, one can reject lockstep loyalties within each of those categories: Be free to move either politically to the left or to the right as occasion demands, *under Christ*, or theologically to the right or to the left, as occasion demands and Christ calls. The polestar that allows for the turn of the wheel is the "one Word of God, Jesus Christ . . . attested for us in Holy Scripture" as the 1934 Declaration of the Synod of Barmen stated it in the "Confessing Church" struggle against Hitler's blood and soil ideology. Its signatories challenged the givens, the culture-war options, in the light of the one Word, Jesus Christ:

We reject the false doctrine, as though the Church were permitted to abandon the form of its message and order . . . to changes in prevailing ideological and political convictions. . . . Jesus Christ, as he is attested for us in Holy Scripture, is the one Word of God which we have to hear and which we have to trust and obey. (The Theological Declaration of Barmen, 3, 1)

The Barmen Declaration has become a model for subsequent movements of protest, large and small. While hardly comparable in scope or consequence, dissenters in the presidential crisis saw parallels on matters of primary allegiance. The "prevailing ideological convictions" of many of us were the policies of our party and president. They appeared closer to the justice and peace agenda of the mainline churches than other political options. What happens then when party and president are at cross-purposes with a commitment to the "one Word"? Freedom in Christ transcends party loyalty and a firm "No" must be said to prevailing "ideological and political convictions."

Vox Populi

In the councils of political decision, what is the weight of the voice of the people? A case can be made that the democratic traditions in the West were influenced by "free church" polity. "No bishop in the ecclesial realm" meant "no king in the political arena." The gifts of the Holy Spirit are distributed among the whole people of God, and derivatively, among the whole people of the commonwealth, not hostage to any pinnacle of power, religious or political. A theological argument can be made for the *vox populi*.

But then comes the question: "when and where?" Is the answer, "always and everywhere"? Not if the foregoing affirmation of *freedom in Christ* is to weigh into the political calculus. What any political power — at the top or the bottom of the pyramid — says or demands is accountable to another voice, "the one Word we have to hear and obey in life and in death." The *vox populi* is not the *vox Dei*.

The questions of identity and priority were propelled forward in the presidential crisis. Allusion was made to them earlier in the chapter on ironies: the odd conformity of some of yesterday's protesters to the popular opinion of today. The lesson to be learned here is wariness of a *polls theology*. This transient voice of the people can never be, ipso facto, the voice of God. Its clamors must be tested by the one Word. The sheer volatility of public opinion in a media-drenched time, a "snapshot of the moment" by the instant camera of the poll-taker, should warn us not to confuse the two voices. Taking such poll figures as the point of orientation for Christian political judgments is to listen to "the voice of a stranger" (John 10:1-18).

Discriminate Judgments

Some say that in the night all cats are gray. Political translation 1: As all politicians are corrupt, they are to be equally condemned, and this fallen arena left behind for the securities of the church and the soul. Political translation 2: As all of us in this dark world are fallen, confess your own sin and do not judge others. Political translation 3: Sin abounds among the powers and principalities. Expect little and settle for a wise Turk rather than a pious Christian.

Reinhold Niebuhr brought his "Christian realism" into the public square with his early *Moral Man and Immoral Society*. It echoed the Lutheran "two-kingdom theory" and sobriety about fallen corporate life reflected in the three above takes on the universal Fall and its political consequences. But Niebuhr was more complex than a single-stream Reformation realism, reflecting his dual formation by both Lutheran and Reformed traditions.[6] He would not take the turn inward to the Christ of soul and church alone, with its turn away from the public arena. Jesus Christ rules both public and private realms. His Calvinist commitments weighed in with their critique of Lutheran temptations to passivity. Yet he brought his Lutheran realism into alliance with these Reformed political instincts. Yes, the public arena is fallen, and the radical love ethic that can be approximated in the personal arena cannot be forced on the public square.[7] The most we can hope for here is a struggle toward derivative norms of justice, order, and freedom, achieved by strategies of power checked and balanced, always acknowledged to be less than what will be in the Kingdom, and so judged and lured by its light.

In those ambiguous struggles, confessed sinners are not immobilized by the knowledge of their complicity in a universal Fall. On the one hand, "in God's sight no one living is justified." All human beings share this common plight. But on the other, "there are sins and then there are sins": a more-and-less must be acknowledged in both personal and social behavior. In the political arena, democracy and fascism are both flawed systems, but

6. His Evangelical Synod of North America and later Evangelical and Reformed church connections brought Lutheran and Reformed streams together in fruitful fashion. See the writer's *Affirmations and Admonitions* (Grand Rapids: Eerdmans, 1998), pp. 37-43, for an argument that Niebuhr pioneered the mutualities of admonition urged in the recent Lutheran-Reformed accord, *The Formula of Agreement*.

7. Neibuhr later qualified his too sharp juxtaposition of "moral" persons and "immoral" society by saying he would retitle his book "The Not So Moral Man in His Less Moral Communities." See Reinhold Niebuhr, *Man's Nature and His Communities* (New York: Charles Scribner's Sons, 1965), p. 22.

the choice between the two is inarguable. Niebuhr described this duality in his Gifford lectures as "equality in sin, inequality in guilt." Later he repudiated this formula, saying he was baffled about how to say that all of us "fall short before God's judgment" but that we must still make "discriminate judgments between good and evil."[8]

Niebuhr's grapple with "discriminate judgments" is a refreshing alternative to indiscriminate calls to "come on down."[9] A fending off of presidential criticism because the critic shares the universal Fall, or has his own record of sexual peccadilloes (Hyde, Barr, and other congressional critics so exposed), cleverly deflects attention from differences in magnitude, venues, and consequences. Knowledge of our equality in sin should certainly temper our furies. Forswearing self-righteousness, however, does not release us from making less-and-more moral judgments. In political matters, all three of the foregoing inequalities — magnitude, venue, and consequences — enter into the moral calculus. Nathan's pointed word — "You are the man!" (2 Samuel 12:7) — to a political figure of another time, David, is a reminder of the "discriminate judgments" that must be made in the public square.[10]

A Post-Constantinian Church?

A cottage industry of literature has been telling us that we are "resident aliens" in a postliberal world. Troeltsch's "sect-type"

8. Reinhold Niebuhr, "Reply to Interpretation and Criticism," in *Reinhold Niebuhr: His Religious, Social and Political Thought*, ed. Charles Kegley (New York: The Pilgrim Press, 1994), p. 513.

9. As in Wall's "Come on Down!" earlier discussed, *The Christian Century* 115, no. 34 (December 9, 1998): 1171.

10. An exemplification of the principle here argued of the relation of personal morality to public office, indeed also about the breach of commandment 9.

option has become *de rigueur* among well-known pastors and teachers in "church-type" denominations, surely yet another irony of the times. But they may be more right than this writer, a long-time critic of sectarian Christianity, has realized. Or so this experience of marginalization suggests. Poll data gave skyrocketing approval to the president's performance, surely influencing his acquittal in the Senate. At the same time the public acknowledged his perjurious actions and counseled "moving on." This "death of outrage"[11] coheres with the charge that we are in the dying days of conventional Christianity.

A lamentation for today's church must include the state of evangelical as well as mainline constituencies. The support of Clinton by spokespersons of the latter was matched in this small saga by the silence of the former. The Religious Right predictably raised its battle cry in this most recent campaign of its perennial culture war. But now we hear disillusionment from many of them; we hear talk of the disappearance of "the moral majority" and the temptations of some to retire to the sidelines of the battle. But apart from the internal debates of political fundamentalism, what of mainline evangelicals? No shouts "to arms!" here. Hardly a murmur could be heard. Indeed, several of their notables accepted the invitation to be counselors of the president, giving tacit support to his professions of penitence. Of course, there were some voices heard from both mainline and evangelical ranks, as evidenced in the Declaration, but *public* sounds were few and far between. (We can hope that pulpits and classrooms proved more vocal and that we may someday find that out from research on this episode.)

Do the sounds and silences mean that it is time again for the catacombs church? For alien residency? The answer must

11. William J. Bennett, *The Death of Outrage: Bill Clinton and the Assault on American Ideals* (New York: The Free Press, 1998).

come from church scrutiny of cultural conditions. One other time and place in the twentieth-century West shows us where the *disciplina arcana* is apt. The "hidden discipline" meant for Bonhoeffer and others[12] that the church must be ready to go underground to preach and teach a resolute orthodoxy and live out a rigorous orthopraxy. Bonhoeffer could discern no ear open to a costly faith in a secular society and a culture of blood and soil. Are these conditions met in contemporary America?

Making the Declaration in the midst of this presidential crisis is a vote against a pure post-Constantinian analysis of our present circumstances. For two reasons: (1) To find at the very center of political power a professing Christian, with supporters sharing that commitment, is to invite a Conversation 1 with those still in the system and affecting its future. While not Constantine, Clinton is no Hitler. A self-defined post-Constantinian church reads itself too quickly out of that crucial future-forming dialogue.[13] While a failed outcome, from the point of view of many Declaration signers, it was a conversation worth having and still possible in ways that would not have obtained in the catacombs of the second or twentieth centuries. (2) To the extent that the charters and codes of this country are still in place, a church with a theology of common grace and moral law can make its voice heard with appeals to those charters and codes. In this case, moral arguments touching perjury, the abuse of power, and the obstruction of justice are apt, and can be heard and were heard and supported by cultural and political decision-makers. To retreat from

12. Dietrich Bonhoeffer, *Letters and Papers from Prison*, the Enlarged Edition (New York: Macmillan, 1972), pp. 281, 286.

13. Stanley Hauerwas, a major exponent of the resident alien viewpoint, signed the Declaration and wrote an important essay in the book. However, he was very clear that he was in Conversation 1, suggesting in his whimsical way that he was more interested in Clinton's being "excommunicated" than impeached. See *Judgment Day at the White House*, p. 31.

this Conversation 2 on the basis of post-Constantinian premises (and with a religious epistemology devoid of universal warrants for conversation) would be an abdication of the political responsibilities of Christian faith, where those political responsibilities can still be exercised. The Declaration acted on that assumption, and a dialogue around its concerns did take place in the public square.

For all the modest possibilities of a second conversation, the presidential crisis reinforces the case for due recognition of current impossibilities. With the diminished influence in Western society of the church and other religious and conscience-forming institutions, sobriety is in order. Yet the mandate for public witness continues, and circumstances do not yet preclude being heard. Because the witnessing church believes that Jesus Christ is risen and rules that realm, whatever the circumstances, no time is bereft of hope of his grace at work in the world of politics, and his call to be present with him there. Even in a mordant moment over the regency of "wrong," James Russell Lowell can give voice to a sober hope:

> Truth forever on the scaffold, Wrong forever on the throne.
> Yet that scaffold sways the future, And behind
>   the dim unknown
> Standeth God within the shadow Keeping watch
>   above His own.[14]

Private Faith and Public Policy

A familiar argument among the signers of the Declaration requires a little more critical attention than it has received from

14. James Russell Lowell, "Once to Every Man and Nation."

cohorts. It goes something like this: repentance and forgiveness are religious matters. Clinton can certainly be forgiven for his sins, however that forgiveness is conceived (unconditional grace with or without response). This religious matter is between him and his God, or his church. What transpires in those relationships cannot be imported into the political arena. Yet, being repentant before God, or among believers, does not translate into absolution for deeds done in the world of governance. In the latter case, different standards apply, and conduct there must be accountable to the norms and procedures of that arena. In Clinton's case, personal professions of repentance do not qualify as substitutes for stipulated procedures and penalties in the *polis*.

Jean Bethke Elshtain made this argument powerfully when she cited the present pope in her essay in *Judgment Day at the White House*. He forgave the gunman who attempted to assassinate him, but did not ask for the removal of the civil penalty for his action. A pastor commenting on the issue drew a similar parallel when he observed that Jesus forgave a criminal on Golgotha but did not ask God to relieve him of the government's punishment. In both cases, an accountability before the law is separated from accountability before God.

In the background of this law-specific argument may also lurk a religious judgment sometimes expressed as, "I can forgive, but I can't forget." In the Lord's Prayer I learn that my own trespasses are forgiven insofar as I am willing to forgive those who trespass against me.[15] All right, I've got to forgive the presi-

---

15. Clinton made reference to just this interrelationship in a parting comment to a press corps inquiry about his attitude after the Senate vote: "If you want to be forgiven, you have to be ready to forgive." The premise of an appeal for forgiveness here is a view of oneself as the aggrieved party, the one who had been *trespassed against*. Thus, his self-defined spiritual struggle was relocated from the repentance befitting his sin; in effect, Clinton appropriated the for-

dent (because of view 1 or 2 above). But that doesn't cancel out the just legal consequences for what he has done.

There is a right distinction here between the religious/personal and the political/corporate dimensions. Human beings have multiple relationships under God commensurate with their existence — as creatures of their biological, social, and economic matrices, on the one hand, and as made in the image of God on the other. The personal cannot be collapsed into the political, and vice versa. Repentance/forgiveness of the soul is not a substitute for accountabilities in society.

While the regions so described are distinguishable, they are, however, not separable. The self is inextricable from society, the personal from the political, the "religious" from the secular. This is so in biblical anthropology and in understandings of the Christian life in soul and society, with effects therefore in the relationships of piety to politics. The argument that what goes on in private before God has no bearing on political issues is only partially correct. It is correct in asserting that we cannot accept religious professions of the heart and mouth — and responding declarations of forgiveness — as exculpatory of deeds done in the political sector, hence the *distinguishability* of the spheres. But Christian repentance entails public acts as well as movements of the heart and lips, acts commensurate with deeds done. Repentant Christian behavior of a public servant requires

---

giveness offered by God and applied it to the problem of his forgiving those he believed had sinned against him.

While repentance is appropriate all the way around, given the complicity of every one of us in this scandal and our common need of forgiveness from God, the president's retort showed once again how religion can be used to serve one's own ends. As pious as the comment appears, it directs attention away from presidential accountability and toward the presumed trespasses of his critics. Thus the burden of his spiritual life is the onerous task of forgiving others the sins they have committed against him!

"fruits meet for repentance" in the public sphere. We have already discussed what those might be.

Drawing the line between religious repentance and civil accountability is also problematic because it can be adduced as support for the larger contention that the personal must be kept separate from the political. The inseparability of the latter is a fundamental premise of the Declaration and of Professor Elshtain's essay, insofar as they pertain to Conversation 2 on matters of a moral "threshold." Consistency of argument, as well as its theological merits, requires the inseparability of private faith from public responsibility.

Sex and Society

"It's nobody's business! What the president does with his genitals is a matter between himself and his spouse. The government should not stick its nose in it. And the public is more interested in getting its problems fixed than Monicagate. Besides, look at all the presidents who had sexual liaisons and nobody ever wanted them impeached. Moreover, they did a good job in governing and it didn't affect their ability to function. The same with Clinton, who has incredibly high performance ratings from the public and is doing a great job. Leave him alone!"

This line of reasoning was pervasive during the presidential crisis. Can it be answered? The way in which a response is made depends on the distinction between Conversation 1 with its specifically theological criteria and Conversation 2 with its broader warrants. We take up each in turn. But not before a passing reference to problems with some assumptions in the above line of argument: (1) If issues of sex are not the government's business, why the demand for a congressional resolution of censure by those who so argued? (2) The fact that seventy million people tuned in to the Barbara Walters *20/20* interview of Monica Lewinsky suggests that the public is more interested in the matter than is asserted by the "Let's move on" constituency. (3) A case can be made that a history of sexual infidelity in presidents is not unconnected with a lack of integrity in the execution of public responsibilities, and also the vulnerability to intimidations because of them. (4) The "Clinton fatigue" that followed the exposure of the president's personal conduct adversely affected the reception of his policies and the political prospects of his vice-president.

Conversation 1

The Christian tradition has a very high view of marital fidelity, as reflected in the rites that launch the union, and the vows taken by the participants. Expressed variously, marriage is an "order of preservation" instituted by God for the sustaining of society, the enabling of humanizing intimacies, and the responsible ordering of sexual drives. Its celebration takes place in the setting of public worship. Thus, in Christian teaching, this kind of "private" conduct has a public face and public consequences.

The church has carried forward in its rites and rationale the ban against adultery set forth in the decalogue. The seventh commandment is part of the "second table" that in both Christian and Jewish traditions has come to represent standards for society as well as for its believers. (The latter is sometimes expressed as the convergence of "natural" and "revealed" moral law.) That is, the violation of the marriage covenant is linked with murder, stealing, false witness, and covetousness as acts that injure the public weal. Thus marital fidelity is not incidental to social health in Christian-specific teaching about a responsible society. While no part of today's orthodoxies, modern or postmodern, it is a long-standing teaching of the church. Why would this norm not apply to a professing Christian at the pinnacle of social power? It therefore has every right to enter Conversation 1 when the president or his religious supporters draw a sharp line between "sex and society," between presidential infidelity and the political order.

Conversation 2

In Conversation 2, the case for one's view has to be made on the basis of public evidence according to criteria agreed upon in a particular public venue. We have a growing body of data on the relation of sexuality and society. It cannot be excluded from this dialogue. David Heim refers to it and draws the right conclusion about its relevance to the Clinton episode:

> Many students of public life, and especially those interested in the health of civil society, have come to realize that so-called private issues of marriage and sexuality have very public ramifications for the stability of families and especially the welfare of women and children. In this context it is a mistake to say, that the loving Christian position is that sexual activity is private and therefore not open to public judgment, or that sex is not as big a deal as politics.[16]

"Sex is not as big a deal as politics" is an argument made in Conversation 2 as well by the Christian privatizers of marital infidelity. The data to which Heim refers make it as difficult to

16. Heim, "Judging Clinton: The Religious Debate," *The Christian Century* 116, no. 8 (March 10, 1999): 279.

segregate the issues of sex and society in public debate as in theological fora.

*　　*　　*

Theology is best done in the midst of the struggles of one's own time. When there were giants in the land, that was always so, not the least in the work of twentieth-century mentors Barth, Bonhoeffer, and Niebuhr. And they did it from within the ranks of dissent.

The call continues in our lesser times and smaller sagas. A presidential crisis — a quarter century ago, and yesterday — can shed light on grace and repentance, the integrity of the "one Word" and the ambiguity of human professions, judgment days penultimate and ultimate. So the effort in theological journaling here undertaken, the better to prepare for the next time of trial, and for the perennial test of faith by its dissent from the cultural orthodoxies of the day.

Appendix

Declaration concerning Religion, Ethics, and the Crisis in the Clinton Presidency

As scholars interested in religion and public life, we protest the manipulation of religion and the debasing of moral language in the discussion about presidential responsibility. We believe that serious misunderstandings of repentance and forgiveness are being exploited for political advantage. The resulting moral confusion is a threat to the integrity of American religion and to the foundations of a civil society. In the conviction that politics and morality cannot be separated, we consider the current crisis to be a critical moment in the life of our country and, therefore, offer the following points for consideration:

1. Many of us worry about the political misuse of religion and religious symbols even as we endorse the public mission of our churches, synagogues, and mosques. In particular, we are concerned about the distortion that can come by association with presidential power in events such as the Presidential Prayer Breakfast of September 11, 1998. We fear that the religious community is in danger of being called upon to

75

provide authentication for a politically motivated and incomplete repentance that seeks to avert serious consequences for wrongful acts. While we affirm that pastoral
counseling sessions are an appropriate, confidential arena in
which to address these issues, we fear that announcing such
meetings to convince the public of the President's sincerity
compromises the integrity of religion.

2. We challenge the widespread assumption that forgiveness
relieves a person of further responsibility and serious consequences. We are convinced that forgiveness is a relational
term that does not function easily within the sphere of constitutional accountability. A wronged party chooses forgiveness instead of revenge and antagonism, but this does not
relieve the wrongdoer of consequences. When the President
continues to deny any liability for the sins he has confessed,
it suggests that his public display of repentance was intended to avoid political disfavor.

3. We are aware that certain moral qualities are central to the
survival of our political system, among which are truthful-
ness, integrity, respect for the law, respect for the dignity of
others, adherence to the constitutional process, and a will-
ingness to avoid the abuse of power. We reject the premise
that violations of these ethical standards should be excused
so long as a leader remains loyal to a particular political
agenda and the nation is blessed by a strong economy.
Elected leaders are accountable to the Constitution and to
the people who elected them. By his own admission, the
President has departed from ethical standards by abusing his
presidential office, by his ill use of women, and by his know-
ing manipulation of truth for indefensible ends. We are particularly troubled about the debasing of the language of public discourse with the aim of avoiding responsibility for one's
actions.

4. We are concerned about the impact of this crisis on our children and on our students. Some of them feel betrayed by a President in whom they set their hopes, while others are troubled by his misuse of others, by which many in the administration, the political system, and the media were implicated in patterns of deceit and abuse. Neither we nor our students demand perfection. Many of us believe that extreme dangers sometimes require a political leader to engage in morally problematic actions. But we maintain that in general there is a reasonable threshold of behavior beneath which our public leaders should not fall, because the moral character of a people is more important than the tenure of a particular politician or the protection of a particular political agenda. Political and religious history indicate that violations and misunderstandings of such moral issues may have grave consequences. The widespread desire to "get this behind us" does not take seriously enough the nature of transgressions and their social effects.

5. We urge the society as a whole to take account of the ethical commitments necessary for a civil society and to seek the integrity of both public and private morality. While partisan conflicts have usually dominated past debates over public morality, we now confront a much deeper crisis: whether the moral basis of the constitutional system itself will be lost. In the present impeachment discussions, we call for national courage in deliberation that avoids ideological division and engages the process as a constitutional and ethical imperative. We ask Congress to discharge its current duty in a manner mindful of its solemn constitutional and political responsibilities. Only in this way can the process serve the good of the nation as a whole and avoid further sensationalism.

6. While some of us think that a presidential resignation or impeachment would be appropriate and others envision less

drastic consequences, we are all convinced that extended discussion about constitutional, ethical, and religious issues will be required to clarify the situation and to make a wise decision possible. We hope to provide an arena in which such discussion can occur in an atmosphere of scholarly integrity and civility without partisan bias.